The Right Course Vs. What's Left

The Right Course Vs. What's Left

Richard Hewitt

Writers Club Press
San Jose New York Lincoln Shanghai

The Right Course Vs. What's Left

Writers Club Press
an imprint of iUniverse.com, Inc.

For information address:
iUniverse.com, Inc.
5220 S 16th, Ste. 200
Lincoln, NE 68512
www.iuniverse.com

ISBN: 0-595-17852-9

Printed in the United States of America

PREFACE

Welcome to the new millennium. As the old saga goes, we may have arrived by different means of transportation, but we are in the same boat now. Whether we permit ourselves to live to the fullest, or as an abbreviated human being is up to us, the citizens of this great nation. Nothing has been promised to us except equal opportunity.

We have been blessed by an ever expanding growth of knowledge, which bodes well for the next 1000 years. However knowledge alone, without wisdom is threatening to undermine, to sabotage, to destroy, and derail the train carrying the cornucopia of good things that can and should be ours, paid for by our efforts to accomplish, which is a reasonable requirement.

Wisdom is the proper use of knowledge. Knowledge without wisdom is a one way street leading to insanity and madness. What is known will one day be done. Science without wisdom will destroy the human race.

Wisdom is not for the intelligentsia alone, it is a jewel that all may acquire and posses. Wisdom is not inherited, it is not given at birth although it would appear that it is at times.

Wisdom can be acquired the hard way by meeting failure after failure wondering why one cannot accomplish, or one can go to the source at a rather young age and acquire it. There is a bountiful supply of it, but it is rarely sought or used, and that is the problem that we face.

It is sincerely hoped that this writing may encourage the reader to search for wisdom after he or she acquires some knowledge, because it will be in a sense a difference between day and night in their lives. This book will reveal the source of all wisdom, and how to approach it and drink deeply of it for a more productive and prosperous life of reality.

We in America as in all nations are directly effected by the thinking and the attitude of the general population, and more especially the leaders. It is the thinking and the attitude of the people that develops the culture, and it is the culture change in America that is going to bring the nation to its knees. The people will get what the people think they want.

There is a great cultural divide in this nation, and those on either side are becoming more and more rigid in the positions they have taken, there is less and less room for reasoning.

On one side are the university educated, and some few who are not, but have the right stuff to make it big and become leaders in industry, and are rewarded with high salaries, On this side are the entrepreneurs, the risk takers who build businesses, builders who employ others. Last but certainly not least these people live by a set of principles that develop character, and inner strength to meet the vicissitudes of life, and when a battle is lost they come back with more determination to win. They detest crudeness, crassness, arrogance, and cheapness. They value life, and a life of value. They ask for nothing more than equal opportunity.

On the other side are the university educated and some few who are not so educated but have the right stuff to build. However the majority are not university educated, and work in manufacturing plants, which is an honest noble endeavor. They find someone to get them a job, and then join a union to keep it. They are the followers, they are not the risk takers, and they certainly are not leader material.

On this side are the militant feminist, who are constantly on the march for their special interest. Their followers generally are capable of thinking of only one thing at a time. They are the one issue people, they certainly are not leaders, except those who lead the leaderless.

On this side are the militant civil righteous whose leaders keep telling their flock never to forget how they were and are being abused while they the leaders are living luxurious lives on the donations of their people. The leaders are mostly reverends and they are clever enough to call their organizations religious institutions and thereby become tax exempt. They collect millions of dollars per year and spend a few thousand on their followers needs. The Jesse Jacksons, the Loweries, the Al Sharptons, Maynard Jacksons, mayor of Atlanta Georgia, and so many more across the nation are keeping black Americans from reaching their potential, because they are heavily indoctrinated with fear, hate, inferiority, and low self esteem. The leaders will never cease from preaching their gospel of hate because it pays well, and they stand in the limelight basking in the admiration of their uneducated followers.

Again on this side are the homosexuals, who no longer ask to be left alone but are now flouting their aberrations as the sexual preference for the race. They now parade with banners proclaiming their pride in their aberrations.

Add to this scenario the trial lawyers who prosper immensely encouraging everyone to sue everyone else and use their services.

This is America and all of the above have a constitutional right to do what they are doing. However these groups have joined at the hip, and all vote for the same political party providing the politicians with a solid block of votes, which is every politicians' dream, and the politicians will protect this special interest block with their lives. Yes, to the point where they are tempted to show more allegiance to the party that provides the life-blood of their political livelihood than to the country, and the citizens they were elected to represent.

This side of the great divide never reaches up for help in order to climb higher, they reach up to pull the other side down to their level, which will result in mob rule, chaos, anarchy, and dictatorship. They reach out for a donation with their left hand, and threaten with their right fist held high. They are the street fighters who will fight and kill if necessary to perpetuate their hold on power. They have been very successful scheming their way into high places, promising to remove every pain known to man, paid for with other peoples' money.

It has been this side that have taken over the governing of the nation, which has resulted in the crassness, crudeness, cheapness of life. This side advocates globalism, reducing the average citizen to the position of serf, an uneducated zombie. The other side advocates a more agrarian philosophy, not necessarily suggesting that we all become dirt farmers as opposed to international trade, but that we become thankful for the beauty of the place in which we live, and revere it.

The two sides are extreme opposites, with neither willing to succumb to the philosophy of the other. The twain will never meet.

Never again will the first half allow the filth, lies, half truths, and downright thieving of the peoples' money to go unchallenged. The second half will never relinquish their hold on the bloodsucking philosophy that has given them all of this power without a fight to the death.

The final result will be revolution.

It appears as though our country is caught up in some sort of stupor, under a spell if you will. We have become under a spell of the experts, the talking heads, and members of the think-tankers, and the University professors, that today the average citizen believes that to disagree exposes their ignorance . We are dumbed down.

The truth being that all of the above experts live in their heads, in the small world of their particular profession, and cannot imagine another world except their own. The worst part of all this is that 50 per cent of these experts disagree with the other 50 per cent. Where do we go for truth? Even the churches have come under the spell of this culture, and are preaching the doctrine of men instead of the gospel of absolute truth.

Our leaders no longer set the example for stability, but quite the opposite, having set the example of deceit, lying, double talk, spin, depravity in action, lacking principle or character, caring only for their personal material gain, chasing the dazzling tinsel of false gold, and false gods in their little world of the Washington D.C. fish bowl, of Wanna-bees.

This work is not to incite, but rather to alert and excite the reader to think and observe so that the people can once again live without undue strain, and live and work in the light, instead of the darkness, and restore this great nation to its rightful position of leadership, not as a braggart, an example of grateful gratitude.

All of this work would be incomplete without my expressing my deepest gratitude to my wife, Norma Jean for the patient hours of listening, and her researching the Internet for facts. Her devotion to the aim and purpose of this work has been a source of constant support.

Contents

WHAT IS NEXT?

The answer to the above question is a revolution. Why? Because the nation is divided and is dividing, and the anger and animosity on both sides is worsening. The nation is slipping and now sliding , and within a decade our democracy of free people will be dissolved in rioting, then chaos, then anarchy, and then the inevitable, some form of dictatorship under the gentle guidance of some charismatic leader who says he truly cares about people, and the people will follow. They will follow, not because they are stupid, but because they trust. and believe that dictatorship cannot happen in America. It already has taken roots in this country, because the basic principles that support democracy are being eroded.

The reason for this is that our government has been turned over to the street-fighters of the urban centers. The Electoral College which is now unfortunately set up to give all of these votes to the winner of the majority should be modified to proportion the votes. A perfect example is New York state, with a population of 18,000,000 with a population in New York City of 8,000,000. Yes, the city itself contains the cultural centers, but it also contains the millions of citizens who refuse to be educated, and the millions who are not educated because they complain that it is difficult to learn in a foreign language or some other excuse. It also contains the unionized workers, who influence someone to get them a job, and then join a union to protect their job. Then there are those who dabble in the arts, and live off the endowments, and are encouraged by Hollywood to produce music, plays, write books that teach irresponsibility with much symbolism but not too much substance.

These different groups are led by the radical black reverends, the gang connected unions that use gang tactics to keep the members in line, the militant feminists, the Gay Rights crowd who no longer ask to be allowed to live their lifestyle, but now demand and parade and brag about their special way. This is America and citizens are free to think and do so long as they do not infringe upon other's rights. However when these groups who usually do not have much in common with one another, join and vote as a block, they control the city and they know it. The politicians know it also, and they bow and scrape for their votes.

These people are Americans and they have chosen what they want to do with their lives, but may we suggest that they are not too well prepared to govern, but they do today through their political party.

It has become almost impossible to be unbiased when one sees the party of one's youth become the party of the street-fighters, casting out any semblance of principle, or sense of decency, or sense of shame, in order to guarantee their permanence in office.

This all began with the F.D.R. administration in the 30s when radical steps were needed to hold the nation together, to avoid riots and chaos. F.D.R. was aware of the danger of big government subsidizing groups and gangs and said so. However politicians saw the great possibility for themselves. Give things away with other people's money that had been collected through taxation. This indeed is a great vote getter.

O yes, the country has two political parties, but today they speak and act very much the same. Both are controlled by the huge international corporations. The corporations do not care too much regarding which party is in power, they contribute equally to both, and they receive their government subsidies from both. The party in power does not any longer govern, it rules the country like a monarchy, it issues mandates, it bypasses congress every chance it gets. It sends the nation's armed forces to foreign lands as peace keepers, nation builders, and relief workers without consulting congress. Of course the congress is forced to supply the resources after the troops are deployed and their lives are at stake.

The aim of the party in power is to remain in power by what ever means is necessary. The end justifies the means. The average Americans are not too much interested in politics, and don't really know how their government is supposed to perform. The politicians know this, so they act accordingly, by adopting an attitude of; "If you can't convince them confuse them". They have done an excellent job of that.

Our presidential elections are now determined in courts and not the ballot box. The courts are now legislating, and establishing new rules as they go along, forcing the nation into the rule of man instead of the rule of law. The citizens of America have accepted half truths, lies, demagoguery, fraud, perjury, suborning of perjury, obstruction of justice, misuse of public property, the confiscating of personal property without due process, low morals, the belittling of religious faith and tradition. After the citizens have been dumbed down, they are then told to be sweet and politically correct in thought and deed, and take sensitivity courses to enable them to be more tolerant of those nasty streetfighters who attack them and take from them their sense of silly decency, and their most precious possession; "The Constitution of the United States of America", which grants freedom, and equal opportunity to all.

When the nation collapses due to the weight of the rule of man instead of the rule of law, and the rioting begins, they will declare an emergency, activate F.E.M.A., declare the separation of power between the branches of government null and void until they ; "The party in power" decides that it is over, and we must remember that F.E.M.A. is set up and always ready to move the professional army in to quell riots and put down opposition when ordered to do so, by the authority in power.

This nation is only a couple of heartbeats away from the above scenario at any time. We must always remember that there is always the private militia groups waiting for the opportunity to test their skills.

All it will take is a little shoving in a crowd of emotionally aroused streetfighters, then a punch is thrown, someone is knocked down, then enter the knife wielder, and the pistol shooter, blood is spilled, a martyr is created, and then the real fun begins. The police will be called to quell the riot, the crowd in its fury and rage will overcome the police and more will die. The National Guard will be called out, and then the citizens who are split politically, in their hate and anger because they are so frustrated with the big lie fed them for years, will go to the streets. Then F.E.M.A. will be called to active duty and that is the end of our Democracy.

Anyone who cannot accept the possibility of this revolution must be a relative of the tooth fairy. The hate, and anger, and the desire for relief is so great in this nation after so many decades of deceit that a revolt would be a welcome reprieve.

The party of the streetfighters will rule the country, and the President of the party will become the benevolent dictator until he says it is safe again for a trial in democracy. His entrenched henchmen will do as they are told as always and proclaim that all is being done in the name of the law backed up by the military, who will do as they are told.

There are well educated, stable and respected people in this country who are at this moment organizing to promote the idea of seceding from the union. Some of these groups are quite well entrenched. They want to disassociate themselves from the filth, the fraud, the two faced hypocrisy of both political parties, and their aim and goal is legal constitutionally.

It is a tragedy for all of us that conditions have been permitted to develop to bring about such a division among our people, who have grown to hate each other blaming their frustration on one another through their respective political parties.

It appears that the only people who do not recognize what is happening are the under- educated, the non-thinking mobs who take their orders from their leaders, or those who believe that they have made it and are above the fray, the completely stupid, or those who just don't care, and would rather return to their cozy apathy.

This is not demagoguery, it is like owning a home to the South of a raging forest fire with a very strong wind blowing from the North. It is doubtful that the citizens would sit in a sense of apathy if the above scenario became a reality.

When in the name of all that is holy, will the citizens of this wonderful country stand up and shout, "Enough"?

The battle-cry of the street-fighters is; "The will of the people", turn everything over to the people and they will straighten everything out, then all will be equal, and fair. The leaders of that party feed this propaganda to the party faithful in order to subject them to their control and power, and more and more of the non-thinking will offer to die for the cause. More and more propositions are now being placed on ballots all over the country, which is a very strong sign that representative government is being trampled on by the howling streetfighters shouting democracy. They don't want democracy, they want their will to be done. If they can't reason out the problem, they will resort to force.

Who can deny that there is a great division between the urban areas, and the suburban and rural areas? One party has the strangle-hold on the heavily populated urban areas, which again contains the poorly educated minorities. Who can deny that there is a great division between the big Eastern States and those of the mid-West, because of lifestyle, traditions, family values?

If one party controls these heavily populated urban areas in large cities they can stay in power forever if the Electoral College is eliminated. The nation will be run by the uneducated, the marginal to say the least. The leaders of this party will constantly shout; "We will fight for you", {you poor uneducated sheep, while we fleece you.}

Fellow Americans, we as an nation are on the brink, brought about by the most deceptive maneuverings ever carried out over any length of time. Even this so-called miracle economic boom was bought with a $500,000,000,000 tax increase on the people, and now it appears as though this miracle is coming to an end along with all of this so-called surplus.

If this be the case what is going to hold us together? Where is the cement, the consensus that held us together for over 200 years, through so many crises, including the Civil War? Are we then to be ruled by the politicians while the two do battle between themselves for power, caring less and less about the country they are elected to serve? These people are elected to be servants of the people not their rulers.

Only the people of our great country can save us from dictatorship. Third parties will always be strangled by the two giant parties. The people will have to organize into large groups and demand to be heard. They must study the Constitution, and ponder the Spirit of the Law, and not only the Word. There must be gatherings in homes and in the granges, in the city halls, and meeting houses to study and learn to interpret. They must then compare their newly learned knowledge with that which is perpetrated upon us by our elected officials and see how far these power hungry career conspirators have strayed from the truth, and their oath of office to perform the duties of their office faithfully to protect our land from all enemies home and abroad. What the entrenched politician fears the most is an informed educated public who understands what they the politicians are doing.

For centuries, no for millenniums, the world had dreamed of the possession of inalienable rights, the inherent rights, the God given rights of Life, Liberty, and the pursuit of Happiness. Not man given but God given. On July 4th, 1776, the dream became a reality in the United States of America, not as a braggart as we are today, but humble, thankful people who demonstrated to the world that freedom is worth fighting for, and dying for. It is this light of freedom that is being extinguished by deceit and fraud, brought about by ridiculing Truth.

We have lost our way, and as a result we have lost our consensus, the delight in being an American, we have lost our vision and are becoming one of the mob of the street fighter nations, we ridicule our traditions as silly bed-time stories for the weak minded, and we have eventually become a post-Christian nation, forgetting that our country was born and nurtured on Christian principles.

It is literally impossible to understand Western civilization without understanding Christianity and how it shaped our culture and even our political traditions.

The United States is an extension of European civilization, and Europe was not long ago known as Christendom, which brought light to a dark world, and even during the "Dark Ages" it was the only enduring light that continued to burn. It was Christianity that brought about the consciousness of the value of human life, the inalienable rights of that life.

Of course today, Christianity is riddled with heresies. There are many more Cafeteria Christians who pick and choose which parts of the religion they will follow and which parts they will discard. They discard those parts they deem to be too inconvenient or politically incorrect.

The idea that religion has to be fashionable is ridiculous. The Eternal does not conform to the temporary. It seems like a foolish thing for people to dismiss religion, when it is certain that science does not have the answers. They have great knowledge, but so little wisdom. It will be wisdom that will hold the world together, not science, it has already proven that.

It is entirely up to the citizens of America, and no one else. This will come as a shock to the majority, after so many years of letting the government do everything for them. Will the answer be a search for Truth, or a continuation of accepting lies, half truth, and deceit. We are not talking about sweetness and light, but about facts, or being swallowed up by them. We are talking about why the shootings at Columbine High School, and other schools. We are talking about other whys that appear to have no answers by the experts, the renowned ones in the think tanks with all of their degrees, who have never lived in the real world but are bloated with theory.

There are answers to all of these questions if one will only face the Truth, and stop strutting around trying to be someone other than what they are, and stop accepting as gospel truth the utterances of the theorists with their answers covered with psychobabble, political correctness, as we watch and see the same ole, same ole.

It is dawn. The dawn of a new hope. It is dawn January 1st 2000. Dawn of a new day, a new week, a new month, a new year, a new decade, a new century, yes even a new millennium. There will be new discoveries revealed by science, better medicine, which is a blessing. There will be changes in transportation, and communications. The world will shrink, and the news of the world will become commonplace. It will sparkle with the newness of things, as it has at the end of the past century compared with the beginning of it. The pace will quicken, will the lame and the halt be left behind?

Who are the lame and the halt? They are the uneducated masses, the poor and the disenfranchised, and those of the intelligentsia who raise so many questions regarding Columbine High School, and too many other calamities. They act as though there is no answer, and are resigned to just talking about it. They constantly mourn for the people who are addicted to drugs, and call it a scourge. Yet they keep appointing Drug Czars, who go about doing the same tiresome things they have been doing for years and years, apparently without a clue as to how to reduce the flow of narcotics into this country.

Why do the lame and the halt keep condemning this present generation as though they were aliens, just arrived from another planet? Why do these children who are given so much by their parents, cause so much trouble and so many heart aches? Why are the parents unable to face the facts and correct the situation? Why do the lame and the halt constantly talk about improving race relations when they know or should know in their heart of hearts that there is a terrible seething and anger just below the surface? Who do they think they are fooling when they approve of new laws that mold and make us a nation of dumbed down, politically correct morons, robbing the citizens of their right of free expression?

The lame and the halt keep asking what has happened to the morals of the nation, the sense of shame, and the sense of guilt, the sense of responsibility that places restrictions upon the citizens in a civilized society. They know the answer but do not have the courage to face facts.

Another facet of the lame and the halt are those who believe that some day they will be lucky and become wealthy, and never dream of preparing themselves to render a service of any kind to their fellow man.

The most pitiful of the lame and the halt are those who are given the answer, and are revolted by it, because it will necessitate a new attitude, and a change in thinking.

With all of the sparkle of the changes of the past century, it must be remembered that it was the bloodiest in the history of the world. The atrocities will not be long remembered in the hustle and bustle of the faster pace of life, in the getting of things.

What will the world do with this wonderful opportunity to bring forth a better understanding of the word, success. Webster's dictionary describes success as gaining wealth and /or fame. An extenuation says; a successful person. It is generally accepted that if one has acquired wealth, fame, or both he or she is successful. This is of course shallow thinking. The world needs less of this type of intellectual musings. Success is the feeling of well being.

What is the world? The world is composed of people and their leaders. The world has the potential for unlimited good. This is so because each individual in it has tremendous potential. The waste of this potential has been appalling, simply because people still believe that in order to succeed, one must be a genius, strut their superiority, develop classes, and be in the right one. The popular notion being, that we must be in competition with everyone else in order to succeed. This is ridiculous. Study the lives of the successful people, Carnegie, Ford, Edison, Einstein etc. and we find that their competition was in themselves, they challenged themselves. Therein lies the human desire to succeed, in accomplishment. Success is not in defeating others, but in defeating one's self, protecting one's self from one's self, defining goals, and developing self discipline in order to accomplish the goal set forth.

All people must be free to dream and do, else none shall be free for long. The world can't hope for peace until the minds of people are peaceful. The horrors of this world are the result of the individual, or the leaders of nations believing the only way to have is to take from someone else who they believe have.

One cannot find peace, living a lie, whether it is a little white lie or a big purple one. A lie is a lie, is a lie, and it reveals the weakness of the perpetrator. Of course the world will always be the home of the lie, because it is in the world that people struggle and strain, defrauding each other, striving for the wants instead of the needs, seeking the approval of their peers. With only a small amount of time spent in observation it is obvious that regardless of the great opportunity available in this country, there will always be those who refuse to take advantage of it. Some because they were not exposed to it by their parents, some because of downright neglect by the parents, but by far the majority because it is easier to beg with the left hand and threaten with the right hand.

It will take more than wishing to make manifest the cornucopia of dreams, because dreams they are until they are materialized, however they can become materialized. The earth on the other hand was created by God. The earth is the storehouse containing every thing to satisfy the needs, not necessarily the wants of His people. It is the striving for the wants that creates the insanity of the world. It is indeed possible to envision a world, where all who spend their labor, spend it in service to others which could be in architecture, engineering, medicine, law, manufacturing or in the most menial endeavors without being tagged with that terrible label, do-gooder.

Who is a do-gooder? A do-gooder is one who sincerely desires to bring one's potential into full view, and watch him or her grow into that potential. A perfect example is a teacher of children. A good teacher is being paid less and less in comparison with other professions, but perform one of the most important services because they are far more interested in doing good, than accumulating money.

The idea of doing good is viewed as antithetical to the essence of American culture today, which appears to be the individual gain of material wealth. There seems to be something un-American about caring for others, rather than making money.

A teacher from Brooklyn who had spent the last eight years teaching in a high school there stated;" the endlessness of the battle to do good was only a burden when he could not see other soldiers in my trench".

Freedom, self-expression, and the individual pursuit of happiness were dreams all over the world, until they became reality in America. These are innate inalienable jewels given to the nation to reflect the brightness of possibility. However she is slowly but surely allowing them to become tarnished. America the beautiful must shine forth as an example to the world, and not a braggart of the material goods she possesses. The world resents America as she brags, and struts, and tells all other nations she is the greatest, do as I do, only we have what it takes. She must remain the hope of the world, not in material abundance but in the abundance of the freedom, and individuality of her people, and their truth. All would say that they detest evil. If this was true, why is there so much of it? Is it because there is so much fear, and anxiety that robs mankind of the nobility to claim his own? Man was meant to be noble, not a slave in any respect, with or without wealth.

The new millennium will bring enlightenment, and hope, not only to a chosen few, but to the world, but only if while building the temple the occupants of the temple, the people, are not forgotten. The temple built with gems becomes an eventual ruin, but the temple built for mankind will last forever. This is not fantasy, this is fact, it is the Wisdom of the Ages, for those who seek it. This is the temple of the soul. It is time to stop thinking like children and mature to the thinking of the adult and become conscious of who we really are. We are not our bodies, nor our brains. nor our minds, because we say that these things are ours. If these things then are ours, who are we? We even claim ownership of our souls. The soul is the magnificent mansion in which lives the spirit of truth or the spirit of darkness. If the soul is taught light the mind will be taught, and the body will follow the dictates of the mind. When the body is taught by the five senses, the soul is darkened. The thought is the father of the act. Enlighten the soul and one's world will be enlightened. It cannot be enlightened by constantly sailing against the wind, by thinking in darkness and proclaiming light, or by proclaiming light, while living in darkness. Seek first the prosperity of the mind, and all the necessities will be added. Pray that the universities will again teach young minds how to think, instead of how to make money.

The challenge of the new century is to enlighten the souls of men and women, so that mankind can live in peace, and bask in the goodwill of others, but not necessarily seek the approval of others. If however mankind continues to search and find only for self aggrandizement it will be much better if the searching and the finding ceases. The shadow of the instruments of mass destruction hovers over the world. Which will it be, enlightenment or cleverness? Enlightenment which is truth can not be compromised.

Every man should be prepared to protect himself, but when the art of self defense is converted into machismo, and worn on the sleeve, and used to intimidate others, this person is not real. A facet of the truth has become tarnished. It is compromised.

It is imperative that the dross of psychobabble, political correctness, and spin, be pushed aside, to enable one to look into the pristine waters and see the truth. Truth the priceless jewel which has been long neglected, remains untarnished. What is truth? This question was asked two thousand years ago by a Roman Governor. It was sincerely asked, as it is rarely asked today.

Truth is an absolute, it permits no shadow of turning, it endures forever. It is the touchstone upon which good or evil, right or wrong can be recognized. Truth is the foundation upon which one can build a full meaningful life, as an individual. It is the only hope in the universe which is capable of setting mankind truly free. Politics and business are temporary, but an algebraic equation lasts forever, because it is truth, it is fact. Why does the world ignore it?

Truth is the quality of being true, being in alignment with reality and fact. The ramifications are loyalty, sincerity, honesty, and trust. Why can't the world accept this? Is it because Hollywood hasn't put its stamp of approval upon it? Or is it the fear of being tagged a nerd? Or is it that one is afraid that all excitement will be removed from one's life? If the latter be the reason for not accepting truth, then their fears should be allayed by the fact that it is very difficult to become so heavenly that one is no earthly good.

Truth is a many faceted jewel, sparkling from the center. It is reflected in all activities of life, be it work, play, relationships, or religion. The truth is not the absence of a lie, because a lie is negative, it drains energy, making one a smaller person. whereas truth is a positive force, an energy, it is light, not darkness. Those who expose themselves to it develop strong characters, they are set free from fear, the emptiness disappears, and they feel whole, and know who they are.

Truth abhors deceit, and cleverness. It shines completely through sophistication, and exposes the shallowness of it. It ridicules self importance. A truthful person is quiet, strong, and steady. A truthful person is in the world, but will not permit himself to become addicted to the cleverness, and the deceit of it.

Yes, there are only few who find it because the many do not seek it. Truth is found in weakness, but when truth is established, weakness disappears, because truth is power. The weakest can become the most powerful, and their life expands.

Shunning the truth has resulted in the subjugation, the manipulation, poverty, starvation, and the theft of freedom all over the world. Look at the tin horned dictators who still strut around the world, flouting their cleverness, and then look at their people.

All can possess this jewel without price by simply seeking the source, the very center of it. It is an individual endeavor. It is an individual choice. The entire world depends upon it.

Although America is the most enlightened nation in the world, it is beginning to show dangerous signs that it is suffering from the acceptance of half truths. Truth cannot be compromised without dire consequences. The gap between the haves and the have-nots is widening. This alone should awaken us to the fact that the American dream is fading, and a class conscious nation is emerging. Throughout history the leaders who proclaimed how much they cared, and then controlled the masses with an iron hand, are legend. They not only controlled the masses, but lived very well during, and after the process.

Even though perfection is not expected, the world can strive for the high calling of truth, and not the low calling of cleverness and self aggrandizement. Cleverness is used to secure power, and power represents the control of people. The corrections require truth, courage and patience.

All endeavors must be supported by an undercarriage of truth, whether they be large or small.

As an example a service station owner, who would be considered an honest person had a decision to make, not earth shattering, but a decision. A customer had come into the station and asked for a lubrication of his car. The owner directed the driver over the grease pit, and began the job.

As he was about to finish the undercar work, he came across a little grease fitting located at the spring shackle. He tried his best to force grease into it, but to no avail after many tries. He removed the grease fitting and replaced it with a new one and tried again, with no success, the pin had rusted solidly.

A decision had to be made, and at that time the owner had no idea how important that decision would be. It was such a little thing. The owner could tell the car owner that he could not get the grease to flow through the shackle joint, and risk the chance that the owner of the car would insist that he try again because no one had ever had trouble before, or say nothing knowing that the lack of lubricant could and probably would wear out the joint resulting in an expensive replacement for the owner. The decision was made. The station owner decided to spray penetrating oil on the shackle joint in order to stop the screeching when the car went over a bump. The car owner would never know. At least he could not blame the station owner months later when the joint finally froze.

After the customer had left, the station owner was left with his conscience. He knew then that he should have told the car owner the truth, regardless of his reaction. He knew that he should have been honest with his customer and he knew he was not truthful. A wonderful thing happened in this case. The owner asked himself a question; What is truth? This started a search that lasted for over fifty years, resulting in a completely new outlook on life. He found prosperity of his mind, which spilled over into material prosperity.

A small matter, but multiplied by the population of a nation could result in a vibrant existence for all.

Every human life is of utmost importance. The human race is the most important entity in the universe. We are the reason that the world was created in the first place. Who are we?

With the very real threat of the fantasy kings and queens of Hollywood, and political correctness, along with herd instinct of so many of the lame and the halt, let us consider what the scriptures says about us.

They teach that we are made in the "image and after the likeness of the Creator". We are also taught that our Creator is King of Kings, and Lord of Lords. Therefore if we are the children of the King, then we are princes and princesses. We are of noble birth, and it is about time we acted like who we are instead of some low life, groveling creature.

It is always our choice. Which will it be? Wait to be fed like sheep, or take control of our lives, and whether we be rich or poor, be the noble person we were intended to be. As the people think, so thinks the nation, and so goes the nation.

A Potent Mix

Human Nature, Politics, and Religion make an explosive mix. Out of this mix mankind has always attempted to establish a sane form of government which would discipline the population, and avoid mob rule, establish sufficient law and order, while promising freedom in the future.

Human Nature

Since the days of the herdsmen, who left the pastures to dwell in cities for protection, there has been the rich, and the poor, the leaders and the followers. There has always been the self interest groups, with the influence to secure special favor from those who govern. This "always has been attitude" is no excuse to continue the abuses. The human race is we hope destined to revelation and light. This does not rob men of their masculinity or the women of their beauty. This will not completely remove the beast within that so many are afraid will happen if we become too good.

There have always been those of the governed who demand answers to their basic questions, such as; what is the government going to do for me, without infringing upon my freedom. Little does the demander realize that he or she has presented for themselves an oxymoron. Of course the more the government does for any special interest group with other people's money, the more mandates there will be, the more bureaucracies established, and the more taxes imposed. It is similar to selling one's self into slavery. The disgruntled ones are both the rich, and the poor. The rich because they desire more power due to a sense of insecurity, and the poor because with few exceptions, they feel helpless, and believe they should be cared for by somebody, who they can eventually hate for not giving more. There is so much education needed, so much more truth needed.

Some of the wealthy have begun to sense an emptiness, a lack of fulfillment in their lives with all their getting, and the poor experience a lack in their lives, because of their constant panic of trying to live from day to day. Some turn to the great philosophers of the past, some to present day mystics, to the crystal ball readers, politics, and as a last resort, they turn to religion of all kinds and zaniness. What is the answer to making all happy all the time? The answer is that there is no answer. It has always been, and it always will be an individual endeavor. Each will prosper in direct proportion to his or her enlightenment. The only demand the people can legitimately make on their government is equal opportunity for all, but not equality, because of their individuality.

The culprit of the mix is human nature, which can be expressed in the most kind manner, or the most monstrous manner. Man left to his own devices is devious, dubious, clever, selfish, and dangerous. This is unregenerate man. The man without enlightenment, a man who may have much knowledge, but little if any wisdom.

The world is full of the unregenerate, who are in a sense predators. They survive by exerting power over other people. All mankind to some degree is painted with this brush. Therefore it comes with no surprise, without bordering on paranoia, that it behooves one to be aware, and careful in whose hands he puts his trust. The deep lying causes, that trigger this condition are multitudinous: fears, low self esteem, emptiness etc. The cure is truth .

If this be the case, why does the world act surprised at the fraud, the unnecessary suffering, and deprivation seen all over the globe? Is the world deceiving itself into believing that a political savior will come along who will right all wrongs? There are at least thirty wars occurring in the world at all times. These are not world threatening at present, but could be. These wars are started and fed by tin horn self decorated dictators, at the expense and suffering of their people in the majority of cases, the fruit of unregenerate man.

All this begins in the dark recesses of the small minds of men who will shun the truth at all costs. The truth will dethrone them. The lack of the truth will keep these nations anchored in the dark ages for decades, and even centuries to come. The lack of truth can bring an enlightened nation, a materially prosperous nation to its knees. This should be the concern of all of its citizens. The success of a few should not, and cannot be allowed to infringe upon the equal opportunity of any. When the value of human life is considered of little consequence, the material success is of short duration, because it has no foundation.

If the exploitation of a nation's resources are used only to provide a better bottom line, higher profits, or stockholders higher dividends, the nation cannot long endure.

It appears that in the midst of a booming economy, there is an undercurrent, a foreboding, a fear of things to come. Too many are beginning to sense exclusivity, while seeking stability, and solidity. They are experiencing an emotion of, it may be here today and gone tomorrow. Things are moving so fast that they resemble an unfinished sentence.

When a $200 printer is considered obsolete in six months, something is wrong. When young people graduate from college, with the sole desire to retire at age forty five, or fifty, something is wrong. How about giving something back? When a C.E.O. receives a $10,000,000 per year salary, and asks his employees to take a cut in pay in order to show a better bottom line, something is wrong.

When large corporations merge and downsize which necessitates the laying off thousands of employees something is wrong. The something wrong is not the large corporations per se, it is the apparent disregard for the individual who is laid off. To the individual who is laid off, it is not just a temporary unpleasantness, it is a calamity. It is true that over the past couple of decades there has been an adversarial relationship between employers and employees. The loyalty factor that existed between the two has evaporated. Today the average employee when applying for a position, or a job, will ask, when can I expect a pay increase, a promotion, a vacation, what are my health benefits, what kind of a retirement program do you have, and if a woman, how much paid time off do I get, when I have a baby? All of these perks cost money, and this cost will of course be passed on to the consumer.

The large corporations on the other hand had developed huge bureaucracies of middle management, which resulted in their skimming the profits to the point where the corporation could not compete in the market place. Add to this the demands of the employees, and one can see that something had to be done.

Therefore the relationship between the employer and employee has resulted in a direct individual negotiation between the two, on a direct market negotiated contract. The employee looks upon the company as Daddy with deep pockets, and the company looks upon the employee as a tool to show a good bottom line for its investors, and nothing more. In fact it appears that if the employee could receive the goodies, and have a constant vacation with pay, they would be content. On the other hand the company would like to do away with the employee entirely, because the employee is always the fly in the ointment threatening to strike and interfere with their world wide plans, which produces huge salaries, and much prestige for the top few. Loyalty has disappeared.

What has happened to human communications, and human relations in all this getting? Has this word success been so contorted that it means only one thing, money? When money, and the accumulating of material things is the sole goal in life, when the seeking of money is done so as to enhance one's power over others, this individual is living a lie. The lie is being lived by the rich as well as the poor.

When the employer looks upon his employees as tools, and the employee looks upon the employer as the fountain of dollars they both are living a lie. The employee in order to establish a high self esteem must develop an attitude that his work is his or her contribution to the society in which they live, regardless of the approval, or disapproval of his or her peers, regarding glamour.

Money is of no value without the attitude of one's desire to serve his fellow man. Money alone is but a means of exchange for services rendered.

The glamour will be witnessed within, with self poise The corporation must develop an attitude that it is there to render a service to the society in which it lives as a good neighbor, and as a good parent it must be concerned with its family, the employees who put their futures in its hands. Is this pollyannish? Certainly it is to those who live believing that the only goal in life is to accumulate material goods, at high speed. Where is the nation going, and why must it go wherever it is going at such a high rate of speed? Where is the consensus, the bargaining table where things can be negotiated, instead of the anger and mistrust of the present condition? No, the corporations will not be converted to sweetness and light overnight, and the employees will not become model employees overnight, but both must stop living a lie, and whether it be the individual C.E.O. or the individual employee, they must stop living a lie simply because the corporation, the employee, or the nation can not long endure. Truth will not be compromised. It is always an individual endeavor, in the final analysis.

Dedicated freedom loving, generous Americans built this nation, not the manufacturer's association, nor the socialistic militant labor unions, or the Bar Association, or the A.M.A.

What is happening to our country when young girls can visit a bar, have a few drinks, cozy up to a young man who meets their fancy for the moment and ask, your place or mine? This is not freedom, it is self imposed slavery, with an eventual loss of self esteem, with all of its ramifications. This is the result of the propaganda espoused by the militant feminists who preach the big lie. It is so easy to want to accept the big lie, when youth cries out for excitement. Of course not all young people are falling for the big lie, the majority are not, but the trend is alarming.

The militant feminists' war cry is: Power. They already have it. It is obvious that when the young girls, and young women, lowered their moral standards, the morals of this nation and many of the western nations lowered. The world is suffering a hangover from the roaring sixties, the hippies, yuppies, who so vehemently, and in some cases violently fought the establishment, are now the establishment, and raising this generation.

This generation of young people is vibrant, much better educated, appear to be more confident than the generations before, when young people were to be seen but not heard. This generation appears to be more knowledgeable, bur less exposed to wisdom. The head-long rush is the result of the energy of youth without the guidance of wisdom. Very few indeed are blessed at birth with this gem, it must be learned with patience. The teaching of the delights of freedom without the imbedding of the necessity of accepting the personal responsibility for each and every thought and deed is a half truth. This is not a sermon on fire and brimstone, it is a plea to use the good common sense, and sense of decency which is inherent in all of us.

Truth will not and cannot be compromised. The result is that this generation is on the fast track going at record speed in the direction of the false god of material gain, prestige, and personal power, with little respect for morals, politics, or society as a whole.

This is not a condemnation of our young people, it is a concern for both them and the nation. The pitiful part of this scenario is that the false god is moving farther, and farther away, and they will have to run faster and longer in their attempt to reach it because of the explosion of technology, and the mergers and takeover of huge corporations condensing the power, which will be held by fewer and fewer people in the higher echelons. A slower tempo must be attained, and a deeper wisdom sought if this generation is expected to survive the creature of their own making.

When it takes millions of dollars to run for public office, and the money is supplied by those receiving favors from the elected, something is wrong. When the citizens are then told that to put limits on contributions is to limit free speech, borders on a half truth. The Supreme Court of the United States has just recently decided that money is money, and is not relevant to speech. The states are free to limit contributions to candidates.

When the Supreme Court of the nation stops interpreting the constitution, and begins legislating, and from one side of its mouth decides that it is legal to terminate a life by aborting, and on the other side of its mouth it declares that if a thug shoots a pregnant woman in the process of a robbery, and kills the fetus, the culprit can be charged with murder, something is wrong. Truth has been compromised. Millions of children have lost their lives as a result. Murder is murder whether it be committed by a thug, or a licensed abortionist. It appears as though the intellectual, the scientist, the educator, and a large part of the great country called America have revisited the Garden of Eden and partaken of the tree of good and evil in order to declare themselves equal in their relationship with God, because of their now great knowledge.

When the post modernists cry that there is no such thing as an absolute truth, and the only truth is their truth as they see it , something is very, very wrong. This is part of the sixties hangover. Should this philosophy prevail it can lead to only one destination, and that is chaos, anarchy and dictatorship. Absolute truth is the only tenant of the soul that will remain firm when all about it is crumbling, the only thing that holds the planets together, the only hope of sanity in a mad world.

Is there no consensus left in the world upon which these self interest groups can negotiate, does the country have to continue to accept these obvious ridiculous half truths?

Again, this is a nation of wonderful people, they are generous, caring, intelligent and vibrant. They are generally healthy, and freedom minded, but there is a deadly virus that appears to be attacking the thinking of these people, and unless it is discovered soon and a vaccine developed, these wonderful people will soon discover that they are no longer free. This will happen because they are told by their leaders that every thing is O.K., and they will take care of every thing, and the people believe.

Politics

The above is not written with an attitude of condemnation, but in a sense of pleading. The leaders of this nation are human, and subject to the same temptations as all humans. Self preservation is the first law of nature, so it is natural for these leaders to protect their careers, some with integrity, and others with what appears to be a complete lack of principles, their modus operandi being that the end justifies the means.

It was not intended that the legislature be composed of career people, but the nation has grown so large, and the governing of it so complex, that it would be a disaster to have part time men and women attempting to govern, even with staggered replacement. However in the meantime it behooves the citizens of this great nation not to believe everything the leaders tell them is right. They must think and speak as an individual, and not as one who is owned by a party, or an ideology. Measure everything that is said by the touchstone of truth. The truth will keep this nation free, or it will succumb to the virus of a deceitful mix of lies and half truths.

It is obvious that there must be organized political parties that spin their ideologies to the people, but the people are not educating themselves regarding the issues, and the politicians know this. Once elected the only thought of these politicians is how their constituents will vote in the next election, and the special interest groups take care of that with their gifts.

The something wrong is the lack of integrity, not knowing the truth and knowing that the truth will set the politicians free, hence the nation. Being politically correct is not being free, it is the stifling of one's honest desire to speak their soul. Political correctness is not the truth, it is symbolism over substance, it is cleverness over truth, it is sophistication over reality.

The nation has now graduated into the next phase of mind control, having to do with hate crimes. One can now be given extra punishment if the powers to be, decide that the crime committed, was committed because of hatred toward a person of different skin color, nationality, religion, and now, or possibly in the near future, a disagreement with an entrenched political party. If the burning of the flag, and lewd pictures of saints are classified as free speech, or expression, why then are the heart felt, soul felt, utterances forbidden?. Next comes the specially trained thought police to enforce the hate crime law. If individuals speak their deepest feelings, and emotions, and this expresses hate, and anger, or the threat of violence, they will become ostracized by society. When will the rulers of this nation learn that morals cannot be legislated, without stifling freedom?

When a percentage of the people of a nation begin to feel that they do not matter, that they are not part of the inner circle, that they are a part of the unwashed outsider group by the C.E.O.s and those in power in Washington, something is wrong.

The something wrong is unregenerate human nature, with its low self esteem, its fear, its anxiety. It is not the searching for the impossible goal of perfection in a lifetime, but it is the striving toward the high calling of truth, which is a process of becoming what one can and should be, to become successful in fact. A nation of successful individuals makes a successful nation.

Politics of course is composed of men and women who seek office, with the proclaiming of their desire to make the country a better place in which to live for all of the citizens. The wonderful part of this seeking and proclaiming is honest in the majority of cases, with these people truly believing that they have a calling to leadership, and many are truly leaders. Again unfortunately unregenerate human nature raises its ugly head.

The newly elected go into office with high hopes of achieving wonderful things. Their resolve is strong. They write bills they hope will be voted into law. Then it happens. They are told by their peers, who are now called colleagues, that they the newcomers, must conform to the rules, and regulations, established by the various committees of the parties if they, the newcomers ever expect to even have their bill considered.

The neophyte is told that in order to get his bills passed he will have to scratch his colleagues' backs. The neophyte is now confronted with a dilemma, he is a person of high character and does not want to spend the taxpayers money on a project that his colleague has asked him to vote for. He simply doesn't believe the project is needed. His colleague explains that he needs the project completed in his district in order to get votes in the coming election. He explains how simple it is, you vote for my project and I will vote for yours. This is pork barrel spending, and it costs the taxpayers billions and billions of dollars per year.

A perfect example is the expressway being built underground in the city of Boston, Massachusetts. It was estimated, that the project would cost about $1.5 billion dollars. It is now estimated that the project will cost $13 billion dollars. The work is halted, heads are rolling, and the project is bankrupt. This little jewel was the brainchild of old Tip O'Neil, the former speaker of the House of representatives, and the Kennedys. 70% of the cost is paid for by the Federal Government, which of course means the U. S. citizens. This project was certainly not included in the national budget.

Are these people evil, wicked, liars, cheats, or dishonest? No, not necessarily, they are in politics, they eventually have to deal in half truths. Unfortunately this kind of reasoning becomes an accepted way of living, and the perpetrator who acts contrary to his or her principle for personal gain is a coward.

Another dilemma confronts the newly elected. He is asked by a lobbyist who represents a large corporation to either vote for a certain piece of legislation which will favor the lobbyists' client, or look the other way and not vote against it. The reward is a generous check for the newcomers' campaign fund in the next election, and the neophyte soon learns how important that is.

This brings up another matter of vital importance, and that is political election financing. This issue must be considered, and dealt with if this nation isn't going to become a nation controlled by large corporations, and block voters, robbing the average, salt of the earth citizen of any meaning to his vote. These people buy the elections. This issue like social security, and Medicare are talked to death, but never acted upon. These issues are difficult to solve and no politician wants to tackle issues that so directly effect the lives of so many people, with ramifications of pleasing the seniors and angering the young who are having to pay the ever increasing cost of the benefits. However these issues will have to be brought up and resolved. Unfortunately it appears that these issues will never be solved because career politicians do not want to solve them, because they use them every election. They would rather have issues to demagogue about than solve them. They frighten people with these issues, and blame the other party for not caring.

The U.S. government is racked by deceit, fraud, and half truths. In spite of this fact, and it is a fact, this nation has the best form of government the world has ever seen, and the proof is in the eating of the pudding. The people of the United States of America are the most prosperous, free living people in the world. Does this give license then to the less than honest behavior of its leaders? The answer is an emphatic no. It does however show beyond a shadow of a doubt, that the citizens of this beloved nation be constantly on the alert to curb the dalliance of these career people, who in too many cases will sell their souls, and as a result rob the citizens of their inalienable rights of life, liberty, and the pursuit of happiness. Thank heavens there is a percentage of our leaders who in spite of being, human, are statesmen and stateswomen, who have a deep love for their country, who would give their lives for its welfare. It behooves the citizenry to exert themselves enough to rise above the sordidness of the present thinking and begin reaching for the light that will expose even more the stench of the carcasses of decay of the walking dead men, and women, preaching deceit. When dealing with human beings we will never reach perfection but we should hope and expect a better tomorrow for all.

It is imperative therefore, that the citizens do not worship these politicians, and must keep a stern eye on their activities. Freedom of the individual soul is at stake.

The constitution of the United States is the bible of our government. The people must raise the red flag when the leaders begin to legislate it out of existence, instead of interpreting it.

Can anyone imagine working for the following company that employs 535 members and has accumulated the following statistics by its employees?

Three have been arrested for assault.

Seven have been arrested for fraud.

Eight have been arrested for shoplifting.

Fourteen have been arrested for drug related charges.

Nineteen have been accused of writing worthless checks.

Twenty one are current defenders in lawsuits.

Twenty nine have been accused of spousal abuse.

Eighty four, in 1998 alone were stopped for drunken driving.

Seventy-one cannot get a credit card due to bad credit.

One hundred-seventeen have bankrupted at least two businesses.

Can you guess which organization this is?

It is the members of the United States Congress. The same group that perpetually cranks out hundreds of new laws designed to keep the people in line. [Source; e-mail info titled, "What a Company"]. One hundred-seventeen of this austere group have bankrupted at least two businesses. Are they capable of running our government? They apparently can not make it on their own, they need public assistance.

Welcome to the human race. It is certainly clear that the smaller the government, the better for all, for so many reasons.

The nation does not only need a reform, because a reform means a change from one form to another, the nation needs to be transformed by the renewing of the minds of its people.

Church

The third item in the potent mix is the church. The word church means the called out. Called out of what? It means called out of the world. How can anyone be called out of the world with out dying? It means one can be called out of the maze of deceit, lies, fraud, self interest, but still live on the planet earth. It is very simple, but not easy, that is why so few try.

Church means so many things to so many people. It is an individual concern and should be. However it is a very important matter because as a person thinks so is he. Therefore as the citizens think, so thinks the nation. The country is bombarded with the cry that we must separate the church and the state. How ludicrous this cry is because whether one is an atheist, a Christian, a Muslim, a Buddhist or a Hindu, as they think religiously is how they will think politically. There is no mystery, all one has to do is look about, and look at how people live in different countries. Note that the countries that have the greatest amount of malnutrition, starvation, and very limited freedom are the countries that have tin horn dictatorial leaders who use their religion to mold the citizens into an unthinking mob. They use the fear of God to keep their people subdued.

America is a nation of diversified people of different beliefs regarding religion. It is imperative that not one of its citizens be deprived of the liberty to worship according to conscience. However each individual's religion cannot be considered legislatively by political correctness or any other ruse.

Consider the word diversity as is presented to the American public The citizens are told that they must learn to live with people of other color, national origin, and culture, in other words the diversity of peoples. This thinking lacks substance. It is a feel-good diversity, which requires none of the complex work involved in dealing with diverse ideas, and points of view.

On that score, sadly, we find a push, mostly from intellectuals and political leaders, for conformity, political correctness, and fearful silence.

The United States of America has a constitutional form of government. This constitution was written by men, who in the majority of cases were Christians. They lived and died by the Judeo-Christian principles. As a result this nation has become the land of the free and the home of the brave. It has become the hope of the world, with freedom for all and malice toward none. The only malice is the malice of individuals.

The constitution very clearly states that the state shall not establish a national religion. This assures everyone not only the right to worship but to worship according to conscience, without fear. It also assures the nonbeliever that he or she will not be ostracized or categorized by the government. It must be clearly understood however, that any facility paid for by the taxes of the people as a whole should not be used for religious purposes of any kind. This places a dilemma before the nation. The dilemma is, that the shining light of truth is being removed from the classrooms, any semblance of the fact that there is a power, an intelligence, authority, greater than one's self is being completely removed by an insidious force working unceasingly to abolish religion entirely in this country, especially Christianity. This force is exerted by those who cannot afford to have their deeds done in the light. They work in the dark, in secret, in devious ways so as not to bring attention to their ultimate goal, which is to eradicate the teaching of the scriptures anywhere in the world.

Rather than turn the light out entirely, and return the world to the darkness of the middle ages, why not develop bronze plaques containing the Ten Commandments, changing the title to the Wisdom of the ages? Allow the students and the world to see how they measure up against reality, and how much they need help.

It must be asked here why anyone or any organization would want to erase forever that which to some is the guide book to life. The answer is simple, they cannot exist in the light of the truth. Who is, or what is this force? In one case it was the will of a mother who objected to her son having to sit in a public school classroom, and be forced to listen to the recital of the Lord's Prayer. It has since been reported that the son has been converted to

Christianity. In this case it was of an individual matter, proving again the greatness of the nation, regarding individual thought, and expression.

However there are several organizations that are exerting very much pressure on all women, which is being absorbed by the young. One of the better known is the National Organization for Women, or N.O.W. If one follows the path taken by these people, a pattern appears very clearly.

Agenda

#1-Equal rights for women.

#2-Equal pay for equal work.

#3-Equal opportunity in the work place.

#4-Protection under law against spousal abuse.

#5-Free love, meaning promiscuous sex.

#6-Abortion without parent's consent or knowledge.

#7-Abortion on demand

#8-Partial birth abortion.

#9-Fathers not needed in the home.

#10-Women's Power.

#11-Divorce is acceptable.

#12-Homosexuality, and lesbianism are simply preferences.

#13-Homosexuals and lesbians should be ordained. as ministers in the church.

#14-Homosexual and lesbian marriages should be considered on an equal basis with heterosexual marriages.

#15-Boys and girls are the same, it all depends upon the toys they play with.

#16-The infiltration of militant feminists into the church who insist that scripture that does not coincide with their philosophy be considered only custom of the time of writing, and not inspired. Therefore should be ignored.

#17-Their close association with other militant groups, such as the militant civil righters, the militant labor organizations, and the extreme liberal groups to form a solid block of votes to force their views through congress disregarding the will of the majority, or the general welfare of the nation.

As a result, the nation is being pulled asunder by these self interest groups. The churches are, as a result preaching a social gospel. The world is teaching the church about morals, instead of the church teaching the world.

Where does one go for a semblance of sanity? The answer is certainly not in human nature, politics, or in the modern liberal churches.

Sanity will be restored when the individual citizen becomes concerned and seeks the source of all truth. Human nature will be regenerated, politicians will have respect for the people for whom they legislate, and the churches will be restored to their mighty responsibility of preaching the gospel of truth to the confused, sick, and dying world, and not the commandments of men.

For this outburst a name must be assigned, possibly fundamentalist, right winger, or one of those, etc.

Cannot this nation once again develop a consensus upon which those with a sense of reality agree?

There is no guarantee of a happy ending in human affairs, or politics. However there can be a happy voyage for those who endeavor to find reality, which is truth. Reality can be and should be the consensus. Although the approaches are many, and compromise necessary regarding the construction of the various paths, what matters is the direction taken by the individual. A consensus held by realists will positively reach the high offices of the nation.

THE MIRACLE BOOM

Oswald Spengler, wrote in his two volume book, "Decline of the West", that Western Civilization would be dead by now.

In all probability the last area of real vitally in our civilization is business and technology. That appears to be in agreement with Oswald Spengler's observation and prediction. He said that our generation would be one of money, dominated by large corporations.

Below are some quotes from Andy Rooney, columnist for the Tribune Media Servicesattms@tribune.com.,5/11/00.

"Mergers are designed to improve profit not product.

Television executives live for mergers, and takeovers. They are lost dealing with the creative people who have to come up with the entertainment which the business people get involved with as an unfortunate necessity. The executives can load a half hour news broadcast with enough commercials to reduce its content to less than 20 minutes. They can and do stuff commercials into a show listed in the newspapers as lasting an hour, until it's down to 42 minutes. Eventually they have to give viewers a little something, if for no other reason than to separate commercials". This is of course fraud. It is dishonest intent. However it is legal. They do not charge for the viewing, except your time which apparently they don't value too highly. The American people are accepting this.

Still even in technology, there is a lot of tinkering and adjusting and improving going on, but there appears to be no breakthrough thinkers like Thomas Edison or Henry Ford, or the Wright Brothers.

Spengler believed "that once old age set in there would be no way to rejuvenate a civilization. He goes on to say, that it might be our destiny, as it has been for other places and at other times, to have been born when something is ending".

Don't be dismayed. Watching the fall of something is about as exciting as watching the rise. People in either circumstance are very likely to be unaware of what they are a part of, since the present always strikes everyone as perfectly normal.

Spengler writes that our age of money would be replaced by an age of Caesars, meaning a return of dictatorships.

Regardless of all the so-called wailing about human rights, it appears that more and more governments are restricting rights, but only to those they find useful. However out there are creative people about to start a new civilization.

Start a new civilization? The Western world will stand aghast in horror at the thought that there can be a better way. To this generation what we have is as close to perfect as we will ever get, it is the normal and natural way.

This normal and natural way is the design of this X generation, whose parents are the baby boom generation. They are robust physically, knowledgeable, vibrant, and give the impression that they are free, and are free thinkers. Unfortunately in their quest for complete freedom, without responsibility, they have sold themselves into slavery of chasing money. which is their only definition of success. This nation, nor Western civilization can continue to pursue and worship the almighty calf of gold, without eventually bringing about chaos, anarchy, and dictatorship.

Robert J. Shiller, a Yale University economist, in his book, "Irrational Exuberance" says that "he believes the stock market is overvalued because less-than diligent investors have unreasonable expectations-expectations not based on careful mastery of relevant research- that earnings will grow extraordinarily fast, thereby producing extraordinarily profits necessary to sustain today's share profits, with their extraordinary price-earnings ratios".

Of course Irrational Exuberance can be bad for the exuberant, and be good for the economy. Shiller believes that the stock market is overvalued, and might swoon, losing one half of its value, creating a decade of stagnation. It is reported that one of Russia's Trotsky followers said about him-" Proof of Trotsky's farsightedness is that none of his predictions have come true yet" However the proof of the headlong rush for money is all about us, and the obvious result is even more obvious.

Irrational Exuberance might be the downfall for the exuberant, and be the windfall for the economy for awhile.

A better civilization will one day arise where production, will be people oriented, and money recognized for what it is meant to be, simply a means of exchange.

All should hope and pray that mankind never ceases to search for a better way. In a materialistic sense man has certainly done that. It is mind boggling to think that in a few short years communications that amounted to human messengers that took days, weeks, at times months to deliver a message, has been developed into instantaneous delivery. Health care improvements have resulted in the life span of individuals from about forty years to seventy five.

With the knowledge already attained, the expansion of knowledge will grow exponentially. Without reaching too far, and with a little imagination, we may see ourselves one day being propelled through space in individual contraptions, considering an automobile to be a thing of the dark ages. We will certainly have much more knowledge, and man will live better and better physically, which is good.

It appears however that the more knowledge we attain, the less wisdom we find to match it. Again, wisdom is the proper use of knowledge. Wisdom is the taking of time to face reality. Knowledge alone is a one way street leading eventually to a dead end, or a brick wall for individuals and nations, for as the individual goes so goes the nation.

This may come as a surprise to some, but the United States of America is changing drastically. The nation will never be the same as it once was. This could be for the better, or the worse, it is entirely up to the citizens in the long run. Better if they think and act now, worse if they accept and live by half truths. It is so simple, everyone knows that all that is material eventually deteriorates, and turns to rust and dust. Wisdom is eternal, and it too grows exponentially. Money is not evil, it is the love of it that dwarfs men's souls. The nation must stop its mad race for the material, or eventually find itself in the category of becoming a third world, has been nation. The shortsighted will bring the nation to its knees. The rapid changes that are being made are being made without the ability or the wisdom to ascertain the ramifications of these changes, over a period of time.

Risking the possibility of being boring, by those of little patience, a short synopsis of an example is in order.

All will agree that this nation is enjoying one of, if not the longest periods of material prosperity in its history. This has come about by the use of knowledge, seasoned with a small portion of wisdom.

The majority of the citizens will remember the famous words of George Bush as he campaigned for the presidency. "Read my Lips". He promised there would not be any new taxes if elected. He was elected, and he did levy an income tax increase on the American people, to the tune of hundreds of billions of dollars. He did this to prime the pump, to create a demand for goods and services, which in turn would create a demand for labor to meet the demand for goods, which in turn would lower the unemployment rate, and raise his ratings. This is old hat, F.D. R. did this back in the thirties to restart the economy. Sadly, when the economy finally shows signs of life the taxes were not, and are not removed, they grow and grow, along with the national debt, caused by the government spending even more than the increase in taxes it had imposed. Raising taxes after promising not to, resulted in President Bush losing the election for a second term, even after his 94% rating after the Gulf War. It was not necessarily the increased taxes, it was the broken word.

The United States has a record of boom or bust economics throughout its history, and the same tired methods were used each time to make corrections, unless there was a war. When there is a bust, the working man, the small business man, and the local farmer pay an enormous price, and the hope of the young people is dashed. No president or no congressman wants this condition to last very long, because it reflects badly on their record, and they will do almost anything to change the situation, even if it is just a temporary cure, like a bandage over a boil.

Now getting back to the changes taking place that will change the face of America forever, and change the conditions of life for every American. These changes are monumental, never experienced before. Unless understood by the people and the leaders, the nation will rush headlong into a collision with reality.

Why are the present times so different regarding the economy, and its effect on the people?

For decades, if not centuries, it was the common belief that there were two ways to grow the economy when it fell into a slump. One was to raise taxes, and the other was to cut taxes. The theory was and is that when the nation goes into a depression, money must be pumped into the economy to create demand.

If taxes are raised and the extra money generated is spent on projects of the elected official's choosing, such as stadiums, recreational facilities, turning forsaken towns into tourist's attractions etc., two things are gained, one was it created employment in the politician's district, which created votes for him or her, and the money received by the worker would be spent for things wanted and not necessarily needed, which in turn would create demand at the factory level, and the economy would grow exponentially. This theory was practiced by the F.D. R. administrations, and unfortunately was so well liked by the professional politicians that it was continued even though there was no depression. It is known as the tax and spend methodology. It is very handy around election time, to talk about.

The result is a tax burden which is out of proportion, the taxes are never reduced because the politicians always have a place to spend more, the budget is always overspent because the administration and congress knew it would be overspent when first adopted. The deficit, which is swept under the rug each year, has accumulated to, (determined by who you talk with), as high as 7.5 trillion dollars, which pays interest to the purchasers of our debt in the amount of $ 354 billion dollars each and every year. It is debt created by over spending. This interest payment would eliminate the problem the politicians are having with Social Security, and Medicare.

After the economy blossoms and the demand increases, unemployment decreases, creating a demand for labor, which in turn causes prices of goods to increase, the dollar loses its value and inflation raises its ugly head. Then the economy has to be cooled by raising interest rates and other adjustments, and the economy slips back into a recession. This is commonly known as demand side economic theory. It is generally the Democrat Party's modus operandi, or economic theory.

They favor big government with huge bureaucracies, employing millions of people who have in some way helped to entrench the party. Their theory is that central national government should control more and more of the nation's business, and social affairs. This is done by constantly mandating controls and regulations, and by so doing more people are employed at the taxpayer's expense, and every mandated social program diminishes individual freedom.

The other method regarding economic growth is the supply side theory. This is the theory advocated generally by the Republican Party. Acknowledging as do the Democrats, that money is the life blood of the economy, their theory does not call for more taxes, they advocate tax reduction, that is cutting the taxes, shrinking the size of government, keeping government out of the affairs of the people as much as possible

Their theory is, instead of increasing the burden of taxes, they advocate reducing taxes, allowing the citizens to keep more of their earnings, which they will save to provide capital for bank lending, or for spending which will create a demand for products, increasing the demand for labor. By doing this the demand for labor increases, wages rise, cost of goods increases, the dollar loses its value, inflation raises its ugly head, interest rates are increased to stem inflation and the economy drifts into a slump or recession.

The Republicans have contracted the same disease of pork barrel spending. They also want to be elected. Cutting taxes without cutting pork barrel which gets them reelected will of course cause the well to run dry. You just can't cut taxes forever to prime the pump without a constant booming economy, taxes must eventually be raised to support the government, somewhere along the way. However the taxes can be lowered after the economic slump is over else taxes will ever increase until they become 100% of our income.

The Republicans are more opposed to the constant demand for new social programs, because they all have to be paid for by taxes. They do not advocate the transfer of the nation's wealth from the worker to the nonworker, by the means of transfer taxes, which is an undercover tax Their philosophy is that if a man asks for a fish and you give him one, he will be back the next day asking for another. If you teach him how to fish he will catch his own, and save his honor.

Now that the two major political parties' ideologies, philosophies, and modus operandi have been compared which have created boom and busts, what is it that has created the most sustained economic boom in the history of the United States, or the world? It is the new phenomenon of cyberspace, which is, the universe of environments, such as the Internet, in which persons interact by means of connected computers. The result being the growth of millionaires, silicon valleys springing up everywhere around the country, and it began to come to the surface about ten years ago. It is just the beginning. Just the beginning, and we have such giants in the field as Microsoft, with its founder Bill Gates already one of the wealthiest men in the world. The general public is becoming enamored, just beginning to understand the marvel of this miracle. The president and the administration nor the Republican congress had anything to do with this phenomenon. It is simply proof of what can be done in America if the government and its tinkerers are kept out of FREE ENTERPRISE.

So again, what does this cyberspace miracle have to do with this pro-longed economic boom?

Back about ten to twelve years ago, George Bush raised taxes to the tune of billions of dollars. He made a deal with the Democrats that for every three dollars of tax increase, they, the Democrats would cut back two dollars in spending. He raised the taxes, and they reneged on the spending. However this influx of tax money, acting as a blood transfusion, was working its way through the economy.

The economy began to slowly expand, but President Bush appeared to sit in Washington, oblivious to the concerns of the people who were being laid off due to downsizing of the large corporations. He apparently felt no need to explain to the people what was taking place, and point out the positive aspects of what he planned.

He apparently felt no need to explain his broken promise, and gave the impression that he was above the fray, and it would be beneath his dignity to apologize. He appeared to believe that the gulf war victory would carry him to the White House, for another four years. We all know what happened.

Now we usher in William Jefferson Clinton, in January, 20th, 1993 as the 42nd president of the United States. His first major act was to ask for a $500,000,000,000 debt reduction bill, which included an extraor-dinary large tax increase. His bill was passed in congress by one vote. Quite a number of congressmen lost their jobs after they voted positive on the measure.

Now, with President Bush's tax increase , and now this huge increase of income taxes by President Clinton, the economy really began to expand, and has become the longest economic boom in the history of the nation, and it is still extremely robust. The economy would have become positive without the huge tax increase imposed by the Clinton administration, due to the technology explosion, but on a more stable basis.

However, the taxes that were raised by Presidents Bush and Clinton are still with us. and will remain with us for a long, long time, if not forever. The politicians despise the idea of reducing taxes, they like to use the issue around election time. Don't solve the problem, just talk about it, it gets votes. The tax dollars well spent by them gets them elected.

Back to the robust economy. After seven years it is not only robust but is expanding. Allen Greenspan, chairman of the Federal Reserve, has raised the interest rate often to slow the economy, in order to avoid the scourge of inflation. The economy ignores the increase and keeps expanding with much vigor.

Throughout the nation's economic history, when interest rates were raised, and the cost to borrow increased, the economy slowed down. Why not now?

The reason is that the technological industry which really began to show itself ten or twelve years ago has developed into the fastest growing industry in the country, employing hundreds of thousands of workers, and it is not effected by the rise in interest rates.

This new industry has been sustained by venture capital, that is investors who gamble their own money in order to reap huge earnings in growth stock. It has been common to hear of some investors earning up to 400 % on their investment. They lend money to start—up companies, and expect no dividend or interest on their money. They gamble that the small companies will grow because of demand, and then they will be bought out by a larger company. In the meantime their investment continues to grow in value and they don't have to pay income tax on their earnings until they sell the stock.

Of course this is a risky way to invest, because the start-up company has had no experience in company operation, and they don't offer any stability, they offer the opportunity to grow rich quickly. However they don't go to the bank to borrow money, so they are immune to interest rates increase.

This get rich quick surge has become an addiction to many, but it keeps the economy humming. However there have been some on line companies go bankrupt recently. The investors who withdrew from the Dow Jones Industrials market, to invest in the technology stocks are scurrying back to the old tried and true. Again however the technology industry will continually bring forth advanced methods of communication, and new companies will be formed with venture capital, therefore not be effected by the rise in interest rates. This is a danger. A short replay would show that under the Reagan administration, taxes were lowered, and the economy boomed, but congress spent more money afforded by the booming economy. The nation was fighting the cold war with Russia, which cost billions of dollars. Our country defeated Russia, but at a tremendous cost in dollars, but not one American soldier lost his or her life. The constant threat of nuclear war diminished.

President Bush raised taxes, then President Clinton raised taxes.

Ordinarily the boom we are enjoying would have slowed down about this time, but the growth of technology will keep it moving ahead for some time in the future, and will not be effected by the rise in interest rates.

Last but not least, the nation owes Allen Greenspan, the chairman of the Federal Reserve Board recognition for his diligent work holding down inflation which would have thrown the country into a chaotic condition. He did this in spite of the fact that the administration pleaded with him not to raise interest rates and tamper with the boom.

The public has been told by President Clinton, that he Clinton is the comeback kid. He has sure proven it with the luck of the Irish, and by the birth of the technology explosion on his watch.

The nation has been dumbed down by half truths for so long that it becomes almost impossible to recognize the lie. Nazi Germany was told the big lie for so long, and so often, that the entire country was caught up in the mania of becoming the master race. This was of course encouraged by the military, industrialists in many countries, who always derive huge profits through the nightmare of war. President Eisenhower warned against this happening in this country.

Our politicians have become so bloated with pride over what they claim to be the miracle economic boom, that they now tell the American people that there is a surplus. A surplus over what? They tell the country that there is no budget deficit now and there is a surplus. To them a zero budget deficit is a surplus. They do not tell the public about the over budget spending that is not mentioned in the budget appropriation. Billions of dollars are spent each year through the back door of what they term over budget spending, like borrowing from Social Security.

Is there a federal budget surplus? See for yourself, check the national debt, and see if its not growing. According to the Department of the Treasury, the national debt at the end of FY97 was $5.413 trillion dollars. At the end of FY 98 it was $5.526 trillion dollars, and at the end of FY99 the national debt was $5.656 trillion dollars. So the debt grew $130 billion dollars in 1999. If we have a surplus, why did we borrow another $130 billion dollars? Check for yourself; www.federalbudget.com/, 4/1/00. As of March, 30th, 2000, the national debt was $5.789 trillion dollars. That is $ 133 billion dollars increase already in FY2000. The Federal Government is still borrowing, and apparently still lying. If asked these questions, the secretary of the Treasury, and about all members of congress would reply in a double speak, which would eventually convince you that you are stupid, and could not possibly understand the intricacies of the Federal Government.

It is vital that the citizens of this nation demand truth before the lies and deceit become an accepted method of dealing with one another. It appears that if you are not a liar, or deceitful you are considered naive in today's world of politics. Why is it so important to know? Because our politicians are like spineless termites, eating the very foundation, weakening our democracy.

They now claim that there is a budget surplus, when they still owe the Social Security Fund billions if not trillions of dollars. They talk about fixing Social Security, and Medicare, while they spend our tax money on pork barrel projects. They talk and talk about the wonderful things they want to do for us, but never get around to getting these things done. Why? Because they know that if they complete any of these things, they can no longer talk about them very long. It is better to hold out the carrot around election time.

How can our lawmakers honestly talk about fixing Social Security, and Medicare, when the largest item in the annual budget is the interest that the citizens pay on the national debt every year which has amounted to $354 billion dollars for FY99 alone. This national debt is the result of unrestricted spending by both parties, covering up for one another.

Compare this $354 billion dollars spent on interest to those who have bought our debt, to NASA with $14 billion, or EDUCATION with only $32 billion, and ROADS with $41 billion. We have already spent $159 billion dollars on national debt interest this year. How in the world in one's wildest dream can any one say that we have a surplus in regard to the treasury of the United States. This is but another lie, told with the attitude that if you can't convince them, confuse them.

It is imperative that one stop here and take inventory, of who we are, and what we have. All of the men and women who serve in the Supreme Court, the Administration, and the congress are fallible human beings with their strengths and weaknesses. There would be few if any who would stoop so low as to steal, to defraud, to earn the title of liar, and not have compassion on an individual basis. These people work hard trying to do the job they were elected to do. What then is the trouble, why is America sliding down the slippery slope into bankruptcy?

The problem is that the citizenry does not know very much about how their government is to operate. They clamor for democracy, more democracy, not knowing that there is too much democracy already. The founding fathers saw the danger in too much democracy, which means the will of the people in domination. They set up a representative system where the people are represented by elected officials who it was hoped would consider an issue in the cold light of reason, not influenced by the emotion, of the mob. Mob rule is terrifying.

Since about 1932 up to the present time, our representatives have deviated from the intent of the founding fathers, and have increasingly listened to the people's demands, by taking polls to see how the wind is blowing, and then navigating the ship of state so that they would have the wind at their backs. This results in pork barrel spending and a weak backbone for our representatives, which we had hoped to call statesmen and stateswomen.

These are not bad people, they are just weak people. They are caught up in a bad situation that is so big and so bad that they can not see how to correct the situation without exposing the whole decaying mess to the people. They fear a revolt if the people knew the truth. So they go along hoping that somehow things will get better. They know from experience that to blow the whistle and resign, they would be ostracized by their colleagues, as poor losers who could not stand the heat, and the show would go on without them.

How can we have too much democracy? Why is it dangerous? Just as a simple example, look at all of the propositions and referendums placed on the ballots at the time of election in many states. The states are encouraging voters to vote direct on issues, and by-pass their elected representatives. This encourages mob rule. It encourages tribal rule. Another method of by-passing the elected representatives is to send troops into other countries without the consent of congress, and to rule by mandates from the executive office.

Today the nation witnesses the million man march of the African Americans, several times a year. Then it witnesses the million women march to Washington by the militant feminists, then it witnesses the marches by the abortionists, and the antiabortionists, then we see the street politic of the anti World Trade Organization, and I.M.F.. And now the nation will be treated to another million mom march by the moms against guns. These are called activists, the do something people. Question? Are these followers of the leaders who lead these emotionally charged groups capable of realizing the long run ramifications of their actions? Are they, or do they sincerely understand the difference between their issue, and how it might effect the nation as a whole? A more frightening question is, do they care? Can they possibly understand that their actions are teaching coming generations, that the best way to get your way is through the channel of street politic, by emotional mob rule. By pass the law, by pass the elected representatives, by pass the Constitution of the United States Of America.

Democracy has been derailed by too much democracy. It is up to the American people to learn about their government, and demand that the nation be again a representative oriented country, before the special interests such as big business, big labor, and the radical fringes take over and develop a nation of haves and have nots, creating a nation of tribes. The solution is simple, not easy. The public must demand the truth. But they will not demand the truth unless they demand it from themselves first. Everyone's self interest is truth in government.

Seek first the enlightenment of the mind, and all of the necessities will be added unto you. And in America one can even seek to own a Cadillac, a mansion, and a large yacht, and have a nice monetary reserve and be honest and truthful earning these things, and be free. We all can have our miracle boom with honor if we but set goals and take the first step in that direction. Our environment is but our looking glass.

THE ESTABLISHMENT VS TRADITION

If one hundred citizens of America were asked at random, to describe America, you would receive many different answers. Some may say that they live in a democracy, others in a republic, or a capitalistic country, or a powerful country. Others may say America is the land of the free, or even the home of the brave. Some may call it the melting pot of the world. If the latter is true, what are we melting, and into what?

What is democracy? Democracy means government in which the people hold the ruling power, either directly or through elected representatives Another definition would be majority rule, or the principle of equality of rights, and opportunity.

In the first definition we have been told that Democracy means that the people hold the ruling power. This is very enticing. to think that the average person can hold such power is intoxicating. This attitude is very dangerous. It is dangerous because it can lead to mob rule, chaos, anarchy and dictatorship.

The founding fathers seeing the great possibility of mob rule, established a republic, where the will of the people is expressed through representatives elected by them. The will of the people expressed through their elected representatives supplies the checks and balances needed for stability. A representative cannot in a willy nilly way vote each self interest group's desires. He or she must consider the ramifications of each vote in relationship with the overall general welfare of the nation. Therefore it is obvious that we do not live in a pure democracy In fact the nation is experiencing too much democracy at this time.

The truth is that America is becoming a nondescript nation. This nation is close to the point where it represents nothing, but bragging about how strong we are, how rich we are. It is losing its high calling of being the hope of the world, the light of the world, the example to the world. Instead of being these things it is becoming hated all over the world, because of jealousy, and its attitude that we do all things better than anyone else.

The nation apparently gives the impression that we are superior. Other nations resent being told by us, how they should govern. If you want to be the big success that we represent, do it our way. Develop larger corporations that devour smaller corporations by buying them out with junk bonds with extremely high interest rates, and then reduce the work force to a skeleton number to cut costs and allow former loyal employees to slip through the cracks and scrub floors or perish.

There appears to be nothing left but the word big. If a nation is not big, or its industry isn't big, or its people are not giants in technology, they are looked upon as prey for the large multinational corporations of America. Those not associated with large corporations are left to take the hind most or what's left.

Where are we going? And again why are we driving to get there so fast? Is there nothing left but money, toys, and things? Are people now considered useless unless they are a C.E.O., or a computer technician building a company which they hope will be bought out by a larger company that was launched only a year ago?

Where in heaven's name is the stability necessary to hold together the nation's foundation. and the general welfare? Or has the term General Welfare become a sissy word to these strong and courageous gladiators who are battling so hard to conquer the trade of the world, and stand with saber in hand and say; " Look Mom at what I have done"?

There is hardly one of these puffed up individuals who would have the intestinal fortitude to face what they have caused so many to face when they merge. What a nice way to say to a person who has spent a lifetime helping the company, that they are now useless, and must be cast into the outer darkness of depression.

Why does this nation spend so much time commiserating about the terrible working conditions in other countries, when the average worker in this country is considered factory fodder by the mighty?

There is a better way.

Alan Keyes in his commencement address to Lynn University graduates, made these remarks. "The mark of a truly great life is a constant sense that there were convictions that mattered and truths that deserved allegiance.

You will go out into this world and you can sell your talents, sell your knowledge. You will sell your time and your labor, but there is not a thing on offer in this all too-temporary world that is worth selling your soul".

Please note that Alan Keyes is admired, and what he says is generally heartily agreed with, but his chance to be elected President hasn't a chance in Hades. The reason is that what he says is the truth, and the people don't want that.

America is selling its soul, and the price it's asking is so cheap. It is so cheap it is gross, and crass. It is selling its soul for consumerism. Yes this nation is addicted to consumption, not the lung disease, but the mind and attitude disease of consuming. We no longer work to supply our needs, we are obsessed with consuming more and more, to satisfy our wants, which are insatiable.

We are now a throw away nation. We no longer repair anything, we throw it away. Automobiles are built with planned obsoleteness in mind. The models are changed just often enough, so that if one takes good care of one's car it will look like a relic in three years, just after the last of 36 payments has been made. All household utilities are in the same category. Computers are obsolete within six months or a year, etc. etc. etc. The really sad thing about all of this is, that the nation now accepts this as natural.

This situation is very good for the bottom line, but very bad for the natural resources of the nation, and they cannot be replaced. The worst part of the situation is that it appears that no one really cares any more, except a few way out radicals.

It is becoming increasingly clear that the United States of America will break apart. The nation has been built upon a consensus on major issues. This consensus is weakening, and the people are breaking up into tribes of self interests. Not only the large corporations, or known organizations, but the people, the general public.

It is ironic, and to some repetitively boring, that in the sixties it was the young who fought the establishment, and today they are the establishment.

As Charlie Reece, columnist for the Orlando Sentinel has so clearly delineated:

The Establishment

It is secular.

It approves of abortion.

It wants an international foreign policy.

It wants a central bank, with a debt based monetary system.

It teaches the citizen that homosexuality is normal, and simply an alternative life style.

It is egalitarian, at least in its propaganda, though in fact it is elitist to the core.

It seeks constantly to remind black Americans that white Americans are racist, and the cause of all of their problems.

It favors a global economy controlled by international corporations.

It favors an open border policy in order to drive down the cost of labor, and break unions.

It favors a centralized government with no restraints on its powers.

Item # 1 Refers to Secularism

To be secular, any entity or organization would not be associated with any church or religion. It is not sacred or religious, it is worldly, temporal, and is not constrained in any way by any moralistic principles.

The establishment is subject to unregenerate human nature, and its fluctuating attitudes of good and evil. The establishment is subject to the whims of mankind whose unregenerate nature is self centered and self serving. It is dangerous to put one's life into the hands of one who is wholly secular.

Item # 2 Refers to Abortion

This is as all who think know, a very emotional issue. This issue reaches into the deep recesses of the soul. It can't be brushed aside with a cliche', or a legalistic expert opinion, because it effects the most precious thing a person has, his or her life. This issue has in the past and is at present, and will in the future divide the nation. There appears to be no consensus of opinion on the subject. The issue is so emotionally explosive that reason is cast out along with about 42 million babies. It appears to be a do or die situation.

The subject must be considered on a reasonable basis, and all ramifications considered. The act of an abortion is to end the life of an unwanted child. This on the surface appears as a very simple solution to a problem. What is the problem? The problem is that to the women who abort their children, find a temporary solution to avoiding the responsibility of the day by day drudgery of the demanding cries of a baby in need. There are multitudinous reasons women give for aborting their children. It could be finances. It could be loss of freedom. It could be the result of promiscuous sex with the little boy who never grew up to accept responsibility. Or it could be that to have a baby would interfere with the lady's career at the time.

Without a consensus based on moral principles there is no hope of solving this problem, and it is a problem because it has to do with who should live and who should die. It has to do with women who for some reason or other have aborted early in life, who now carry a sense of guilt, for the rest of their lives. This is contrary to life itself, it is contrary to the hope of ever having a feeling of well being. It will take years of reasoning, educating, and a strong desire on both sides to truly understand the fright, the fears, the guilt, the shame, the circumstances of others to begin to ease the hate aroused by the emotions that this decision of the Supreme Court has rendered, not discerning nor having the foresight to see the ramifications of its decision, abortion on demand, abortion without limit.

Item # 3 Refers to the Establishment of an International Foreign Policy

The establishment demands this as a must, in order to do away with the nation-state. It demands that the United States of America become global in all respects, including becoming involved with the world's problems and wars. We are already in Bosnia, Kosovo, Korea, Iraq, Haiti, and it appears all over Africa.

The United States of America must of course be concerned with the problems of the world, and do all it can as an individual nation to help avoid war and its horrors, but not have its hands tied by treaties that are signed today and abrogated tomorrow.

This nation is not like other nations. There is not another country in the world who as yet can come close to the understanding of the term inalienable rights. Our constitution is based on these rights. Other nations have adopted what is considered democracy, somewhat patterned after our form of government, but these governments did not conceive of the reality of the freedom for the human soul as did our founding fathers.

We were considered naive and are still considered naive because our founding fathers dared to believe that men could be honest and therefore free. This nation is considered naive in the realm of morals, by the rest of the world. They claim we are like children when it comes to the subject of sex What they don't see is that this nation has not as yet descended to their level of depravity.

The United States of America is in a true sense a second Jerusalem, a nation set on a hill, reflecting the light of freedom to the world. It was and is destined to be an example, and not just another empire, governed by wealth, and self aggrandizement. The nation is blessed with abundant resources, and was protected on the East and the West by oceans of water. We were self contained and were able to prosper and grow into the most powerful nation in the world, surrounded by nations whose kings and dictators feared our success. We did not accomplish this by copying the ways of Europe or any other region of the world with their intrigue, deceit and sophistication.

Again this county must be involved with world affairs, and trade with the family of nations, but not on their terms and conditions. Not on the terms and conditions of the United Nations, or any other international organization. There is not a nation in the world who will not take all we will give, and we are a generous country, and after we have exhausted our resources not discard us like a worn out garment. All of the treaties in the past have been broken to some degree or other, or have been bypassed. Our friends of today are our enemies of tomorrow, and our enemies of today will be our friends tomorrow.

Freedom demands eternal vigilance. Be an example. Speak softly, but carry a big stick. This nation does not need to have its hands tied by international treaties. Why does the example have to become one of the undergraduates. We do not have to go ballistic about globalization.

Let us not be led astray by those who can live only by acquiring power. We are already involved in the W.T.O., the I.M.F., the World Bank, Nafta, Nato, and the United Nations which has bungled just about every operation it has attempted to wage.

The new kid on the block is the [OECD], or The Organization for Cooperation & Development. The purpose of its being is to increase taxes in every country in the world. This may be difficult to accept but it is true. There are nations like France, and Sweden, and other smaller countries that demand that the world raise taxes because that is the only way that their country can avoid a revolution. The revolution would be brought about by the citizens of these countries when their government benefits are reduced. They brag about their one or two months a year vacation, and their four day work week, and their pensions etc. Their taxes are as high as 70%. There are senior citizens who march with banners stating; "Please do not lower taxes". It is madness.

This is why so many of our politicians bring attention to how high other countries' taxes are, and we have no room to complain about ours. They want us to follow the leaders like France and Sweden, which are both on the border of socialism.

Consider Nato, the North Atlantic Treaty Organization, established for mutual protection against communist aggression which has now become a world police force. It now invades sovereign nations, bombing cities and villages, killing innocent civilians in the name of saving the lives of a chosen people, apparently not understanding the ramifications of its acts.

The flimsy excuse our nation has given for the foray into Kosovo under the banner of N.A.T.O., causes one to ask; why don't we bomb Russia for their present foray into Chechnya where the people simply want their independence from Russia? Just kidding of course.

The above is not written with the idea of denouncing everything our government does as it may appear. It is written in a sense of amazement that so many world wide organizations have been created and the average American not having the foggiest idea why they are asked to back membership in them. Who organized them, and for what purpose? Do we know? If we don't, where do we go to receive an honest answer.

The benevolent thoughts of those who advocate the one world philosophy, may appear lofty to some in high places, but in reality they could in their zest for the good of the world, and world trade, be wrong and not fully understand the ramifications of their endeavors.

This nation appears to be hung up on experts, and intellectuals. It has been wisely said, that many an expert is a failure one hundred miles from home. And intellectuals prefer cosmopolitanism, which may be described as a form of universal treason to everywhere. People should realize that intellectuals are the least-reliable source of information there is. They are a people who choose to live inside their heads without regard for the place where their body happens to be. They completely miss most of life. As the Buddhists say, such people are born drunk, and die dreaming.

If the nations of Europe want to unite and form a united states of Europe, so be it. This is being done to compete with the United States of America, regarding trade. Already the French farmers are demanding more subsidies so that they can sell their products for less, and this is just the beginning.

However we can never overlook the fact that the jealousy of some of these nations is very much alive, and nothing would please them more than to see this great hospitable nation be brought to its knees. If this appears to be a bit paranoid, let us not forget that we are dealing with people who for hundreds and hundreds of years have depended upon deceit, and cleverness to survive the deceit and cleverness waged against them They are past and present masters of the art. What do they have to offer?

Why can't the U.S. sit back and let the United States of Europe develop, and work out the kinks like we did, but be on the alert regarding their military build-up .There is nothing we can do about it any way.

We must always be a good neighbor. It is imperative that we trade with the world, but not on the world's terms and conditions tying up the hands of our nation with treaty after treaty in order to enhance the opportunity for the international corporations to expand into other nations, claiming that by so doing they are helping the American worker. The large corporations encouraged by our one world politicians have already shipped about all of the manufacturing jobs to foreign countries.

We already have a $ 70 billion dollar trade deficit with China, which of course means that we are buying $ 70 billion dollars more from China, than they are buying from us. It appears that we do a good job supplying jobs for the Chinese, the Japanese, and the Mexicans while helping the corporations become larger and more powerful.

General Smedly Butler stated; "Imperial wars are a racket, fought by poor boys and girls for the benefit of rich corporations" President Eisenhower stated; Beware of the military, industrial complex in this country.

Is the above a condemnation of all of our large corporations, and shouldn't they be allowed to expand? Emphatically no, and yes.

The danger lies in the fact that they are powerful and exert a tremendous pressure in Washington D.C. lobbying our representatives, and forcing the hand of the executive branch with their money and power.

Again the danger is in the secretiveness in which they operate, keeping the fact that they demand and receive subsidies amounting to billions of dollars of taxpayer money from ever reaching the news media.

A fair question here would be to ask the average low income wage earner, the low middle income wage earner, the middle income wage earner, the high middle income wage earner and the high income wage earner if they know anything about all these treaties, and organizations, except what they see on T.V., or read in the newspaper.

It is vitally important that the people know and understand what is going on within the loop of Washington, and the board rooms of the large international corporations. The people's lives and well being depend upon knowing.

What is the I.M.F.? What does it do? What is its purpose? Who benefits from this organization? Where does the money come from? Who decides who gets what? What are the terms and conditions under which loans are made? Who is the money given to in the borrowing country? Is it given to some dictator who will promise anything to get his or her hands on the millions, or billions of dollars to feed his or her army well, so that it will be loyal to them when they decide to invade a neighbor's border, or put down a revolt because its citizens are suffering from malnutrition? Are the terms and conditions of the loan so severe as to make it virtually impossible to meet? If the loan is not paid back, what happens? Does the I.M.F. threaten to turn the debtor nation over to the world collection agency, or does it invade the debtor country and take its pound of flesh in real estate? If it is decided that the loan cannot be collected, who pays the loss, the taxpayer in America, or the member nations?

This nation's foreign policy is based on the good health and welfare of large corporations.

These questions should be asked regarding all of the above world wide organizations, because in some instances, when a venture went wrong in an investment in another country by a large international corporation, the U.S. guaranteed the loan or the investment, which of course meant the taxpayer pays. This is done through the Import- Export Bank by which the generous taxpayers grant, guarantee below market loans to the large corporations' overseas customers. And by means of foundations they manipulate the American political system.

Our international trade today is to encourage large international corporations to invest in foreign countries where they can exploit the uneducated workers, and then establish a market for their goods. The goods then are shipped back to this country and sold to Americans. These corporations dream of the day when all of this will be tariff free. Many of them are receiving federal subsidies, and tax breaks.

There can be no objection to us buying Chinese products, and they buy ours in fair trade. This is not being done. Congress is, in the name of trade policy, creating new sweat shop zones for the American corporation so that they can exploit the poverty, and the and the lack of freedom around the world.

It so happens that many of these questions regarding I.M.F. can be found on the internet; at www.imf.org. The I.M.F. is associated with the World Bank in a loose way, but information about the World Bank is like trying to find hen's teeth.

Thomas Jefferson stated; Stupidity and Freedom can never exist together.

The concentration of power in the hands of the government, working behind closed doors is anathema to freedom,

James Madison stated, that the states should do 95% of the governing, and the Federal Government should be strictly limited to those powers, and duties explicitly spelled out in the Constitution. The chances of this happening are slim, but Americans should never accept or approve of something just because it exists and is powerful,

Who are they who advocate these treaties, globalization, and organizations? They are generally good people, hard working people, people with vision, they are adventurous people who want to live life to the full. They set goals and meet them, and their dream is building, whether it be in architecture, or building a business.

Are they then to be condemned for dreaming and doing? Certainly not, they make it possible for the average citizen to live with many of the things that they at one time thought was completely out of the realm of possibility. They have lightened the load for many. Our nation is great because of them. They are the true leaders of the nation, and in some cases of the world. However we can never forget that they are human, and have their weaknesses as do we all, and some live within their heads, and forget there is a world out there, a world of people who are effected by their leadership, who do not live in their world.

Let us not find ourselves in the position of the people of a small village in Russia, mentioned in the book; Brothers Karamazov, written by Dostoevski. The people of the village were executing a man, by burning him at the stake. When the stranger drew closer he saw that it was Jesus, the Christ. He shouted to the people and asked, Do you know who you are executing in this horrible manner? They replied, yes we know who it is. The stranger then asked why. They answered him and said; Because He threatened to set men free, we don't want to be free. We want to be led, and told what to do or think

This is America today. The American people have been dumbed down by political correctness, demagoguery, lies, half truths, and deceit. The politicians, and the C.E.O.s know this instinctively, if not consciously, it is a part of the mass psychology gleaned from study, or through observation over many years of association with people of various intelligence levels.

Good biology, without good philosophy will result in a calamity. A foreign policy without a good philosophy will result in misery for billions of people all over the world.

The world is more apt to be destroyed by bad politics, than bad physics. Only the truth will keep our nation, and the world from becoming a cesspool from which emerges the dictators.

Let us all remember that capitalism itself requires a certain level of honesty to function. Functioning without the restraint of morals, capitalism can be as brutal as communism.

The nation has a difficult time getting the smartest, best-informed, most ethical people to take government jobs. Most Americans who have distinguished themselves, and become well known in some other field wouldn't consider running for office.

Item # 4 Refers to Central Bank with a Debt Based Monetary System, and Usury

The Central Bank, or the Federal Reserve Bank which has its home offices in Washington D.C., was established in 1913 It has 12 branches in various sections of the nation, because the people in government thought that the nation's money was being concentrated in only one area of the country.

The Federal Reserve holds money for other banks, and lends them money for very short times, at a very low interest rate.

There were, and are times when commercial banks lend out too much money which puts them in a difficult position. The difficult position is that if too many people for whatever reason decide to draw their money from the bank, the bank could not meet the demand, which would cause a panic, and a rush of withdrawals.

Any bank can become a member of the Federal Reserve by depositing an amount of money with it, the amount determined by its size, and general conditions.

As an example; during what is now known as black Tuesday, or Tuesday, October 19th, 1987, the stock market plunged 508 points. The Federal Reserve notified all of its branches to lend money to all reputable stock brokerage houses as they needed it. They did this of course because they saw a national panic if the investors all over the country decided to sell their holdings, and demand cash. The public was not made aware of this happening.

The Central Bank is authorized to audit the books of any and all member banks to ascertain whether the bank is holding sufficient reserves.

The banking industry, and the nation learned an everlasting lesson, when in 1929 the stock market crashed because of the domino action that took place.

Back then the market was wide open. There were no restraints. It appeared that everyone in the country became an investment freak overnight. One could buy stocks with only 10% down, the economy was very good then, and the people thought that Utopia had arrived. They bought just about any stock that was pitched to them, and then they would brag about how smart they were. They made real estate investments all over the country without seeing the property. They bought building lots in Florida that was touted as ocean front, or on the water, when in fact the lot was at the bottom of the bay or the river, or in a marsh.

This is a very familiar scenario as we witness the mad rush to make a killing in the stock market, buying shares in the many start up companies who have not established themselves, simply waiting to be bought by larger start up companies. However there are some restraints now that were not in place in the roaring 20's.

Back then the banks thoroughly enjoyed the mad rush of business, and kept lending money on these fluky deals that in no way could be represented as collateral. On a sale price of $ 50,000 for a property, the bank, loaned $ 45,000. The terms of the loan demanded that if the property showed a depreciation in value for any reason, the borrower would have to pay the depreciated difference in cash. Some just borrowed more from the bank, because the borrower had other assets to be used as collateral.

Others, or the majority did not have other assets, and could not pay the assessment. The bank had nowhere to turn. The property when appraised was shown to be about worthless. The bank lost the amount of the loan, and had no collateral to sell to recoup its loss. When the bank was audited it was shown that its reserves were in poor condition. The banks appealed to their political representatives to keep the auditors out of their banks, blaming them for the hearsay that was beginning to circulate. The depositors of the bank became nervous when they heard the rumors, and began to withdraw their funds.

This developed into a panic when depositors lined the streets trying to get inside the bank before all the money was gone. Finally the government had to step in and close the banks until an audit was made of all banks, and only the banks that showed any sign of stability were allowed to reopen with a guarantee to the depositor, the beginning of the F.D.I.C.

With the majority of the banks closed, with people having lost their savings, and with businesses unable to borrow money to operate, the businesses shrunk and shrunk, until they did not have the funds to buy, or wait until their creditors paid them, because they were in the same sad position. Yes, some did jump out of windows, and others sold apples on the streets. The unemployment rate became 25%, and the populace was in despair. Military veterans marched to Washington D.C. to beg for the bonus that had been promised to them, so that they could feed their families. They were routed and shot at.

This was the beginning of the great depression of the thirties. This depression never ended until the U.S. began manufacturing war materials for Europe, and our soon to be allies in World War Two. This revival of our economy began in about 1939 when Hitler invaded Poland drawing in France, and England according to the mutual protection treaty that these countries had signed.

So we see again the greediness of the money changers in the temple of the trusting people. As a result, restraints were applied to the banking world to keep the unscrupulous from repeating the offenses of the past with other people's savings. The government now guarantees deposits at any member bank up to $100,000 per account. The banks are audited regularly making sure that there are sufficient reserves The loans are also monitored to insure that there is sufficient collateral to support a loan, and that there is no hanky pank between the bank officer and the borrower, who may have political connections, that might be helpful to the bank.

It is imperative to remember that this $100,000 deposit guaranteed by our government, means that if the bank is so mismanaged that it must be closed, the taxpayer is really guaranteeing the depositor's money.

Today's America with all of its great knowledge, but little wisdom, claims that was then, and those things cannot happen to the enlightened people of today.

O ye of little observation, vision, and short memory. It was only in the 1980s that it happened all over again. The only difference being that this time the fraud was with the Federal Savings and Loan industry. The fraud was brought about when nationally known developers prepared fraudulent papers, with fraudulent appraisals, and presented them to the local Savings and Loan for a loan in the millions of dollars. The name of Keating should ring a bell, as he was one of the most prominent developers, and con- men. The Keating five included five prominent U.S. Senators, and the Speaker of the House of Representatives who told Mr. Gray the president of the Federal Home Bank Board to keep his auditors out of his state.

The officers of the Savings and Loans, the appraisers, who raised the value of a property to meet what the bank demanded, in order to make the big loan, received big bonuses.

Of course this cesspool collapsed under its own weight of corruption, and cost the taxpayers of this nation in the neighborhood of $ 300,000,000,000. Yes, the nation survived, but the industry died because of fraud, lies, half truths, which are just waiting for employment in another industry.

Restraints had to be implemented by the Federal Government because people in high places in their small minds believe they are so superior to those sheep who work, save their money, raise a family and put their trust in the people in high places.

Let us never forget that every restraint placed upon us reduces our freedom Lies, half truths, deceit, and fraud, is slowly leading this nation into the prison of darkness, dictatorship, and suffering of its people. Now is the time to take time to read, read between the lines, listen, and listen between the lines. Think of the ramifications of each issue, pro or con, but for the sake of all that is freedom do something and don't just sit there and let it happen.

What is happening is not new, it has been the same since the world began. However with all of our acquired knowledge isn't it fair to assume that we will be smart enough not to let it happen again, and again? Human nature has not changed, but with wisdom we can change it, to avoid repeating the dark ages all over again.

The above shows that lies, half-truths, and fraud lead to restraints that slowly but surely rob the nation of its freedom.

The other half of this issue is that the establishment advocates a Central bank with a debt based monetary system, and usury.

The government budget is so often compared with a household budget. This is not necessarily a good comparison, but on the other hand it simplifies what could become a very lengthy and detailed discussion.

When the nation was very young, naive, innocent, and noble there was one thing that was not permitted, and that was debt. Debt was considered a shame, it denoted instability, and an inability to manage one's affairs. Even after a war, or a disaster, the first thing done was to pay off the cost of the emergency.

This held quite true up until about 1932 when the great depression broke. As was mentioned above, money was used to prime the pump, in order to restart the economy which was in a sense a last resort. The money was government money printed for the purpose, and that of course became a debt to be paid. The W.P.A. or the Works Program Administration, which put men to work cleaning up the roads, shoveling dirt from one side of the road to the other, and the C.C.C. or the Civilian Conservation Corps that enlisted men to work in the forests and country side on environmental projects were paid by government money. This continued for many years, even to the approach of the war in Europe.

The economy was so weak that the citizens could not be taxed in order to pay the debt so the debt remained a debt, and was swept under the rug, year after year, and interest was paid to those who bought the debt, but the debt remained.

After the economy improved due to our beginning to produce war materials for our soon to be allies, the politicians were not slow to pick up the idea of deficit spending. They began to spend over budget, and the deficit was swept under the rug. This has been repeated year after year. Only once or twice was the budget ever balanced, but the national debt under the rug was growing, and interest was paid to the individual, the companies, the banks, the foreign nations who bought our debt.

The repercussion of this type of leadership has been a $7 trillion national debt which is under the rug, the accumulation of years of deficit spending. The cost to the American taxpayer is $354 billion each and every year in interest payments to the investors who have bought this tremendous debt. In connection with this is the over budget spending our leaders do not talk about, goes into the general fund to be spent as the whims of the leaders dictate.

Another ramification of this type of leadership is the encouragement the young people are receiving to borrow themselves into debt. The entire nation is afflicted. The debt is not the result of buying what one needs, but buying what one wants, and cannot afford. What will happen if and when the economy goes south? Who will be stuck with the worthless debt?

No nation or individual is free when enslaved by debt.

The Central Bank is closely associated with the Treasury Department. The Treasury Dept. accounts for the money in circulation, and safeguarding the treasure of the country.

The Central Bank is responsible for ordering money to be printed to meet current needs of the economy. As mentioned above the Central Bank is authorized to raise interest rates to control inflation.

The Central Bank works independent of congress, and the executive branch of the government, it is sometimes called the fourth branch of the government.

Our nation and our people are debt ridden. This is not a healthy condition for either. There are no reserves against a sudden reversal. The savings by the citizenry is now negative, there is on the average more individual debt than savings.

As truth wanes, derision begins. Truth is like Dawn Dishwasher Cleaner, it moves scum out of the way.

America is developing into a cesspool of untruths, and downright lies, and has a need for a high volume of Dawn-like remedies.

Item # 5 Refers to Homosexuality

The establishment wants people to think of homosexuality as a normal and alternative lifestyle.

What is homosexuality? Webster defines it as having sexual desire for one of the same sex as one's self.

This subject is of course emotionally charged. Those who practice this lifestyle plead with those who don't, to try to understand the love that exists between two homosexual partners.

Straight couples can indeed understand that a true love can exist between two people of the same sex, but when it comes to sexual desire, they stand back as though the lights went out, as though something short-circuited.

Why do they do this? Is it because it is so unnatural? If it is felt that a thing is unnatural, should that person be told by those in authority, in the schools, universities, and government bureaucracies to accept this lifestyle as just another way of having sex? It is also added that by no means should this sexual lifestyle be considered unnatural. Those who advocate this way of life say that we should all love one another, and be friends, regardless of our differences. It could also be part of the dumbing down of America, making us into a sort of mush to be molded more easily.

Without going into the titillating aspects of the subject, one does have to visualize what one would have to do to have satisfactory sexual relations with one of the same sex. Some of the ways could be quite revolting to those who do that which comes naturally.

Should the straight people condemn the homosexuals, abuse them physically, or emotionally? Of course not. Should the homosexuals be permitted to establish themselves as a minority and demand special rights? Of course not.

All know that there are many aberrations at birth, that the average citizen hears nothing about. Boys are born with the genitals not fully developed, and the doctors remove the genitals so that the individual can function as a female, However, the testosterone remains, and the little girl becomes a bit rambunctious at times.

The doctors, and psychiatrists at one time said homosexuality was a learned lifestyle, and could be changed through therapy. They now say that they are not sure.

There are hundreds, if not thousands of former homosexuals who leave and denounce the lifestyle and say that they became involved through experimentation.

Who knows the answer? On the other hand, what difference does it make? If homosexuality is an aberration at birth, that is a burden to bear for the individual, but like the boy whose genitals were removed, it is quite likely that he will not suggest that his condition be termed just another lifestyle, to enable him to declare that he is a part of a minority which should receive special political consideration. If homosexuality is not an aberration at birth, then it is a learned lifestyle, and can be changed.

In the meantime it is suggested that the homosexuals do what they do in the privacy of their own bedroom, and stop passing themselves off as an abused minority demanding that their lifestyle be accepted on a par with straight people.

If homosexuality is a birth defect then the individual should be pitied for having to carry such a heavy burden through life. However the homosexuals do not see it that way. They organize into groups such as " Gay Pride", and Act Up, and parade in the streets with an arrogant attitude. The first amendment grants the right to free expression. Free expression can be a blessing or a curse. It all depends upon the attitude and the aim and goal of the one who claims they are abused, or neglected.

Marching in the streets can be a blessing or a curse. It all depends upon the attitude of the marcher.

Marching gained the women's vote. Do we have more honesty in government? Marching brought about prohibition, with its associated gang wars, and loss of jobs. Marching in the streets has brought about the civil rights nightmare, that appears to have no end. A million Mom march to Washington to ban guns has been energy lost, it could have been better spent staying home talking to their children.

Marching in the streets during the Vietnam War gave comfort to the enemy which was communism, and wounded this nation so severely that its wounds will take many decades to heal.

Marching in the streets by the homosexuals will fool some of the politicians into believing that their organized vote is important, but in reality they represent a very small percentage of the population, but they are teaching the young, that to be broadminded and with it, they should accept this lifestyle as just another lifestyle.

Item # 6 Refers to Equality

The establishment is egalitarian in its propaganda, but in fact is elitist to the core.

When the word egalitarian is dismembered it reveals the meaning to be, Equality. This word with all of its emotional feel good is one of the most misused, misinterpreted, most dangerous words in the English language. It has been used by kings, dictators for centuries to arouse the mob to do their bidding. It has been used by scoundrels since the beginning of time as a last resort to arouse the mob to overthrow the government, or invade another country to seize their loot, for themselves.

An example is the French Revolution. They shouted fraternity, comradeship. brother, patriot, and equality, as the promise that all would share equally in the new France. As a result, heads rolled, and blood ran in the gutters. It took years before the killing stopped. The idea was to kill all of the present leaders, and anyone affiliated with them. They would clean the slate and start all over again, with all being equal. Of course it never happened, because it can't happen. It is a physical impossibility for all to be equal.

Another example is Russia. The Bolsheviks stirred up the mobs all over Russia with the promise of equality. They then murdered the King and Queen, and all of their children, and anyone else who was loosely associated with them. With the threat of authority removed the scoundrels took control of what they called the government, and the people were relegated to taking orders from the perpetrators who kept promising the people equality after another five year plan was accomplished.

The Bolsheviks were very clever, they propagandized the world into believing that at last equality had been achieved in their nation. They built a subway which was considered a state of the art achievement, and displayed a facsimile at the World's Fair in 1939. They feverishly pursued converting Americans to Communism, by having their agents setting up cells all over the nation. Their war cry was, "Workers Unite", while their workers were not permitted to unionize, and yet thousands of our citizens were converted. Their axiom was, give according to ability, and take according to need. Doesn't this sound wonderful? It sounds just like equality. The only problem was that human nature raised its ugly head, and the needs became wants and there was not enough to go around.

The leaders lived like kings, while the people lived on promises of equality.

There are millions in this country who believe that socialism, and communism is the ultimate good, and the only reason that it did not work in Russia was the wrong leadership.

Our leadership is shouting democracy, equality for all, elaborating the beauty of diversity, while they with their C.E.O cohorts are living in their private estates like kings. They are elitist to the core while they promise equality in the near future. It can happen here. It is happening here. Beware of those who sell equality.

Equality is impossible because of our individuality. We are not equal physically, or mentally, or emotionally, along with the fact that we all did not experience the same background or environment. The more people know the easier it is to learn more.

Item # 7 Refers to Racism

What a disease of the mind, for that is where the problem lies.

The establishment seeks constantly to remind black Americans, that the white Americans are racist and the cause of all of their problems.

No one can deny that the blacks suffered physical, and emotional pain, and their dignity, their self image, their sense of identity was destroyed when children were separated from their parents, husbands separated from their wives, destroyed by the curse of slavery. They were lost souls, not of their own making.

The Emancipation Proclamation left them unable to read, they had no skill to offer the market except working the land, they had no place to go but back to their former owners for a handout, and the former owners offered them a status of share cropping, which meant that they did the same work as before, but now had to pay their own way from the share of the profit that the former owner established, plus hand me downs from the owner's family.

The big lie was told so often, by the elite, that the citizens of this nation came to believe that the Negro was sub-human. This of course helped to alleviate the sense of guilt of those who enslaved other humans, for personal gain.

However, history shows that slavery existed throughout the history of man. Some slavery was and is self induced in order to borrow money to pay debts. Slavery is being practiced in the country of Sudan today. The black leaders are today selling their people into slavery to Arab countries. Why do we not hear of this practice? Is it as Madeleine Albright states it when advised that Christians are being persecuted in the Moslem world, including The Sudan, that the issue isn't marketable in the U.S.? Is she saying that these issues have no relevance regarding politics?

History teaches that Rome conquered Greece. Then the Greeks conquered the Romans through their democratic inclinations, which resulted in the beginning of representative government in Rome.

England was a barbaric country, until conquered by the Romans and Roman law imposed. The Irish were indeed barbaric until an Englishman by the name of Patrick, who was taken from his home by an Irish raiding party, taught them the ways of civilization. All have heard of Saint Patrick.

As awesome, and foreboding as the words conquer, and conquest might be, the nations conquered benefited immensely through their suffering of subjugation. Future generations have come to live in a civilization more humane than their forebears.

As wrong and inhuman as slavery was and is, the American black has been given an opportunity to partake in the greatest experimentation of freedom known to man. If they had remained in Africa there is an excellent chance that they might fare as poorly as their countrymen do today. It is time that the American black community stop demanding more and more. They are about to kill the goose that laid the golden egg.

If the issue of race is so injurious to them, why have they become so racist?

The black leadership is the arch enemy of their people. They constantly remind their people that it is whitey that causes all of the problems. It is profitable to have a large contingent of followers, look at Jesse Jackson and a few other reverends who are leading their flock into darkness. Jesse Jackson is a millionaire.

The N.A.A.C. P. was at one time one of the most stalwart organizations in the country. The National Conference on the Negro, which convened in 1909, led to the founding of this organization There were many thousands of Caucasian people who were concerned about the plight of the Negro after slavery, and contributed regularly to the cause.

Today this once dignified edifice of concern for all, is now a hotbed for radical rantings of the black community, its finances drained by the officers in the practice of fraud.

Beginning in the sixties, during the Johnson administration, with its Great Society Program, trillions of dollars of tax money was spent building new apartment buildings for those who were living in the slums, and the ghettoes. They were granted a small income, food stamps, and health care benefits to help them get started realizing the American dream. They moved into these new buildings, and received their dole, and food stamps which they used for their wants instead of their needs. They began to realize that if they had a baby they could receive more money, so they began to have babies. Having babies with no sense of responsibility

kept these people in slavery, as they became pawns for the politician, who used them as their secret weapon to get the black vote.

The women had their boy friends who kept them pregnant, and then disappeared leaving the women to cope with raising a family, while they went about bragging about what men they were.

It would appear that those in the black community have little ability to manage life's affairs. How can they when they are constantly told by their leaders that if they had received the forty acres and a mule as promised by the Federal Government after they had gained their freedom, all things would be different today. This has become a new demand by some today. Whose forty acres would they take today? Would they plow the land and follow the mule if they were given forty acres, or would they sell it and buy a new car? These people are constantly reminded how abused they were and are.

They have purposely developed an attitude of arrogance. When the mayor of Atlanta, Georgia, Maynard Jackson, told the black community to stop grinning, and shuffling like a nigger, the blacks did stop grinning, or even smiling, and developed what to them is the bad look. Their purpose was to intimidate the whites, to give whitey something to fear. The tactic worked. The blacks now not only demand, they threaten. The Muslim community wants to establish a nation within a nation, of course a nation of Islam.

These people are wandering in the wilderness. They have false leaders who say I am He, follow me. False prophets leading their people into forty more years of the wilderness of stereotyped existence.

Martin Luther King through sacrifice accomplished much, through his teaching of non-violence, and would have been the true leader of his people if he had lived. The black community has today separated themselves from his teachings, and accepted the more radical leaders who promise to get more things done for them quicker.

Whitey is no longer the stone wall standing in the way of the black community, it is a sickness of the mind of the people.

The black community is seeking identification. They have a terrible fear that whatever they do will result in failure. They fear being stereotyped as being stupid. This has been proven ridiculous by too many people of the black race. However it is no solace for those who are cursed with thoughts of inadequacy.

It is a terrible thing when anyone gives up and doesn't try or tries to cover up their fears with an attitude of superiority accompanied with arrogance.

When a member of the black community tells you that the black children in some of the black churches are taught that stealing is wrong except if you steal from whitey, because they took all that belonged to you, this disease of racism and hatred will never end.

When a black taxi driver from Nigeria with a masters degree, who speaks five languages tells you that the American blacks believe they are too good to drive a cab, who is being hoodwinked?

When the punk in the street can intimidate an eager young person who wants to learn, and cause him or her to quit trying because of a threat of becoming a whitey, racism will continue to control the minds of the black community.

If you do not know anything it is hard to learn at all. This is why it so hard for those of little learning to fare well in school. The more you know the more readily you can learn something new. The smarter you are the smarter you can become more easily, in spite of the fact that some are born with superior intelligence

In other words a core of knowledge must be established if one wishes to rise up out of drudgery of mediocrity. There is a difference between children of the rich and poor, because the children of the rich are more prone to learn more from their parents whose vocabulary will be greater than that of the poor child's parents.

Racism can never end until there is a core of knowledge established in the black community.

William Raspberry, who happens to be black, and is a respected columnist, wrote in the Fort Pierce Fla. Tribune, Fri., June, the second.; At one extreme, some black kids in the inner cities refuse to study, or permit their peers to study because academic exertions is acting white.

At the other extreme, hard working black college students, many of them from solidly middle class families, have trouble performing up to the level of their ability.

Stanford's brilliant black psychologist, Claude M. Steele isn't casting about for an academic-sounding way of blaming Whitey for black failure, his theory comes out of his work, a fascinating series of experiments which can not be done justice in so little space.

Steele's theory is that black students are inhibited by the threat of being viewed through the eyes of a negative stereotype, or the fear of doing something that would inadvertently confirm that stereotype.

Both Steele and a University of Texas psychologist Joshus Aronson administered difficult tests to two mixed groups of black and white students. The first group was told that the purpose of the test was to see how smart they were, the second that it was only to measure their experience with problem solving.

The whites in both tests fared about the same. The blacks on the other hand who thought that their intelligence was being tested scored significantly worse than the others. Steele theorizes that the first group feared to confirm a negative racial stereotype.

This is a serious condition for all of the citizens of this nation. This mental condition of the blacks is causing a division among us. Racial hatred is not subsiding, it is growing more intense, but deeper in the psyche and will continue to become more intense until the black community's leaders stop lying, and covering up the truth, telling the blacks that they are being abused by every facet of the American society.

This is nothing more than making excuses for the punks who deal drugs, the muggers, or the so-called sports bums who have turned baseball, football, basketball, and hockey, into a brawling mob, with its crassness, and crudeness overshadowing the spirit of sportsmanship of clean physical competitiveness.

This is why the blacks have been stereotyped, and the decent hard working, hard studying black citizens have to bear the brunt of the lying by their so-called leaders. They are the culprits.

It is about time that the black community stop calling themselves African-American, and become Americans. The suffering of their forefathers has presented them with a golden opportunity to become what they wish to be, if they know who they are. If they wish small they will remain small in their own minds. It is up to them, it is not up to society to baby sit them any longer.

Let us hope and pray that the leaders of the black community will inspire their followers to be all they can be, and stop nursing them with poison milk.

If their color bothers them, they are going to have to learn to live with it. It doesn't bother decent Americans, their only concern is how to live with the arrogant attitude and the self pity of those who follow the leaders who betray them.

This country has spent forty years, and trillions of dollars in an attempt to integrate the black community into the American system. The black community is now trying with all its might to segregate themselves from the American Way. Let us hope and pray that this reversal doesn't take another forty years and other trillions of dollars of taxpayers hard earned dollars.

It appears that the so-called black leaders are following the culture of the tribal chiefs of old. These leaders had absolute power, and were ruthless. They were the chief of the tribe until they died, and they knew that could become reality at any moment. There was always someone in the wings waiting for a sign of weakness. The people adjusted and did what they were told.

Today in America the leaders are not threatening their people, they are retaining their standing as chief among their people by lying, and arousing the people to follow them in their constant demand against society because of past history, instead of encouraging their people to achieve on an individual basis, and plan for the future.

Item # 8 Refers to Multinational Corporations

The establishment favors a global economy controlled by the multinational corporations.

One of the most dangerous possibilities of this or any democratic nation is the formation of a military-industrial complex. The formation can be and usually is insidious. It starts out innocently enough with no modus operandi for pursuing deceit or the seeking of raw power, but this is a natural inclination when one forgets human responsibility, and reaches out for the world's kingdoms, or if a deal goes bad. The military follows the dollars, and the young men and women who serve so patriotically die, or are maimed to support what they are told to die and be maimed for just like the civilians who are not told the truth by our leaders.

Therefore it is better to stop, think, analyze, and stand up and let our concerns be heard now rather than after it is too late to disagree with the dictators who will follow.

Americans are so trusting, and this is a good trait, and a healthy mental condition, however this does not mean that we become sheep and be led by the unscrupulous to the slaughter of our freedom.

Americans say that it cannot happen here, when in fact they do not seem to care one way or another. They do not vote, or get involved. They appear to be far more interested in just accepting the Status Quo.

America is pulling itself apart with multitudinous self interest groups. The nation is ripe for a strong leader who will take control, and promise peace and quiet in five years.

Fascism is a three legged stool. Its base rests on a combination of government, military, and industry. The tools are nationalism, with a large portion of patriotism, which is used by scoundrels, as a last resort to arouse the masses to do the bidding of the war lords.

Under Fascism, large corporations are not taken over by the government, however the government dictates what they produce, and the quantity of production. The government promises the corporations labor peace by controlling the workers who are not allowed to unionize, and are not allowed to change jobs without permission from the government. A powerful military is developed and the war machine is supplied by the corporations under government control. The masses, the populace, the people, are considered being owned by the state. Scapegoats are established to take the minds of the masses off their loss of liberty and freedom and concentrate on their hate, and patriotism.

It appears that our government, and the large corporations will get their way regardless of what anyone thinks of it.

At one time it was only the individual nation that was effected by the curse of fascism, but we must now consider the possibility of it happening here, and as a world empire. In the name of freedom for us and our posterity, America arouse yourself and be heard before it is too late.

If the nation, if the good people of America, would for just a few moments cast out every particle of superficiality, they would find a sea of pristine beauty. radiating from the facets of the jewel of truth. Yes, when all that is unreal is removed, there remains only one thing, the unaltered truth, and the truth is worth fighting and dying for. If one does not have something to die for, he or she will really not have anything truly to live for. With all of the folly of men, the truth still sustains life, and will supply the only hope of man living with other men. Oh, what a lofty outlook, so impractical, so naive, such child like thinking, so say the soothsayers of the world who are so wise in their own conceit. These trained mechanics of narrow minds sincerely believe they can control the world markets and lift humanity in the process. These great minds, these capable minds have gone to school to learn to make money, and they have succeeded. They should be complimented for achieving their goal, however this does not qualify them to rule the nation, effecting the lives of millions of persons.

The world constantly appears to be trying to find the answers to some thorny questions, but when it comes to facing the facts, reality, which is truth, it flinches, and ridicules, and begins to label, call names, and refers to some damned fool they call an expert, who is a failure a hundred miles away from home with a few degrees embroidered on their sleeves who they hold up as the true one. Some of the biggest damned fools are the intellectuals who are now teaching our young people to be damned fools, by teaching young minds utilization instead of civilization, as part of their curriculum.

The American public is constantly being told, that they must get with it. They are told that we are living in a new era, and if we don't get with it we will be left behind. What is it that we must get with? It appears that it is the same group of moderates who have been carrying the torch for a half century to form a world wide economy, tearing down tariffs so that corporations can trade more freely. Is this what it is all about, and the citizens must get with? The moderates have been mentioned because a moderate is one who stays in the middle, and is agreeable to everyone's opinion, They consider themselves to be nice people who do not want to offend, so they go about in their sweet way of voting, coercing, persuading, and if the situation permits they will pull the rug out from those who disagree with them to get what they want but would never think of demanding it. As the scripture puts it; You are not hot or cold, you are insipid, and therefore I will spit you out of my mouth. This wonderful nation was not built by moderates.

Is it our patriotic duty to throw our hats in the air and shout bravo when we do not have the foggiest idea of what these stalwart leaders are advocating?

There is no question that the people who are driving for a world economy are very smart in their fields. They are leaders in their fields. They have built large companies by producing products and services which have in the majority of cases been a boon to the nation. These people are generally well educated, well disciplined, and have a singleness of purpose. They get things done. They are Americans, with many having fought in the front lines when the nation was at war. They have and love their families. They are generally very decent people. However what does this have to do with the subject?

As is commonly known, a person can be all of the above, and yet be very small. A small mind is a wonderful thing to waste. Without directly associating these talented leaders of industry with the unsavory likes of Trotsky, Stalin, Hitler, we must ask; where are you attempting to lead our country?

These dictators had dreams of grandeur. But for who? Giving them the benefit of doubt, and say that they had good intentions for the people, they made grand mistakes and brought their countries to their knees, and the people suffered. They proved one thing, and that is that it is a dangerous thing to place the nation's welfare in the hands of a few men, scheming behind closed doors, and especially when they have the politicians in their pockets bought by large international corporate money by their contributions. It is plain stupid to go along just to go along without understanding where one is going. The detailed plans of these leaders must be spelled out for all to see.

If asked to do this, the reply would be, that you the general public wouldn't understand the intricate workings of a large corporation, so be like the sheep, going before the shearer, open not your mouth.

This is not a matter of politics, it is a matter of freedom for the people of America in the long run. Be informed now, not after it is too late to complain, and be hung by the neck for being an enemy of the Fatherland, or the Motherland, or the Fairyland.

It is imperative in society that a man and wife provide, and protect their home and loved ones. The concerns of the world must be considered at a much later date, after the concerns of the family are met. Let us protect American families first. Only the truth can do this.

After that outburst we can expect the usual reaction, and reply. That is; get with it. Stop your preaching. That stuff is all right in its place. The place for that stuff is in the church, not on Monday in the business world. You do not understand business, only we of the higher echelon of C.E.O.s. know what is better for the people. Well, let us examine this concept.

Beginning at least with the Nixon Administration on through the Clinton Administration, the nation has been bombarded with T.V, newspaper, and radio ads singing the praises of N.A.F.T.A. They preached this North America Fair Trade Agreement like the old time preachers preached the Bible. In both cases the people listening didn't really understand what was in the text, but it sounded good and made one feel good.

The fruits of the treaty are now coming to light. The American sugar farmers in the state of Florida, mostly in the Everglades have been receiving subsidies from the Federal Government for years, encouraging them to produce sugar. This year it will be the same. The farmers want sixty million dollars for their surplus sugar, which amounts to about 20 cents a pound. The market price is six cents a pound.

On top of that, Mexico, according to the treaty, will be permitted to ship 250,000 metric tons of sugar to the United States without paying one cent tariff. Whether she does or not, it is a threat to the American farmer.

Is this a reward to Mexico for the privilege of shipping auto parts, and other parts to Mexico to be used to build cars, and other things, at lower labor costs, which are shipped back to the U.S, reducing the demand for

American labor, with the large corporations not having to pay tariff either way?

Back in the beginning of the century, John D. Rockefeller the president of the Standard Oil Company, looked at China with its huge population, and stated; I see a market in the filling of the lamps of China. What is wrong with that statement? There is nothing wrong with the statement per se, the question is, did Rockefeller see an opportunity to supply a need to the peasants, who could not afford whale oil, or did only dollars signs dance in his head? This is not a condemnation, it is simply a matter of attitude consideration.

The house of representatives has recently voted to grant China permanent favorable trade relations. This is a big money issue, and big money usually wins in Washington. Then to add insult to injury, they established a so-called watchdog committee on human rights. This committee is to oversee the execution of the new trade relations. What a joke. The U.S. has been scolding China for years about her sweat shop labor, which of course makes it impossible for American labor to compete with, hence China manufactures goods with slave labor, and the U. S. buys U.S. goods made in China. The big companies tell us what a break the U.S. citizen is getting, by being able to buy China's manufactured goods at so low a price. We buy from them but they do not buy from us. We buy our own goods back from China. The result is a $70,000,000,000 trade deficit with China. Is the trade deficit with China, or with the international corporations? There is no objection to trading with China, the objection is that American workers are laid off, because our big corporations are cutting deals with China to manufacture American brand name products with cheap labor. Economics 101 has always taught that labor is the biggest cost to a corporation, so one may ask; what is wrong with big business shipping the high cost of labor overseas? There would not be anything wrong with this if it did not lower the living standard for the American worker, whose job has been eliminated.

If this international trend continues, and manufacturing is done with slave labor abroad, who in the long run is going to be able to buy the goods from China or any place else at any price, except those in high paying jobs in Silicon Valley. We are burning up our resources, and closing some of our manufacturing plants and shipping our raw materials abroad to be manufactured by sweat shop labor, and then we are told how we are providing work for the poor people of these third world countries, and teaching them new trades, and the wonders of democracy. The greatest fear for these humankind loving individuals is that the economy in this nation does not go south or into a depression. With manufacturing plants closed, and citizens unemployed, there will be rioting in the streets, and it will take the army to restore order, not the police and the national guard, which have always been there in the final analysis to save the rear-ends of the instigators of the suffering of the masses.

The baby boomers, and their children, the X generation are a spoiled lot having never seen anything that resembles a real depression. They have never had to face facts, or reality, or truth. They have been pampered, humored, and spoiled, and given things to make up for the loving family they never had, and have no idea of what they are missing, but yearning for. They will not put up with a depression, they will either commit suicide, or riot because someone has taken away the toys that they have been taught to believe are a natural divine possession.

Labor unions in this country have pushed and pushed, and demanded and demanded so much in the past, and became so powerful, that it got to the point where they could shut down the country. They pushed so hard that they have now driven the manufacturer to seek an answer to their problem, and that is how to compete with the world with such high labor costs. The labor unions are not naive, innocent abused organizations, they have been, and will continue to be brutal in their demands, because of the dictatorial leadership, not necessarily the individual worker. The unions are killing the geese that are laying the golden eggs. It is obvious that things are not as they appear, or what the international companies would have the American people to believe. What a tangled web we weave when we practice to deceive.

What our international corporations are now doing in China, they are doing around the world. There is hardly an American product that is bought by the American public that is not made in another country with cheap labor.

Just recently a man's jacket, not including a vest or a pair of trousers sold for $235.00 in a nationally known department store. The label read, made in Taiwan. This is not a discount type product. Why wasn't it made here?

We have been lied to about Haiti. The U.S. sent troops to this country to help to establish peace in the country. The leaders permitted all of the trees to be harvested for their profit. There was and is about 75% unemployment, with no help from anywhere. When the people try to escape and go to another country they are either drowned during their voyage, or turned back. And the American public is told what a good job we have done there. The murder continues.

The textile industry in this country could not meet world competition because of unionized workers. They now spin the cloth, make the patterns, and ship both to Haiti, where the fabric is sewed by slave labor, workers willing to work all day for a dollar or starve. If a mistake is made in the pattern it is shipped back to the U.S., corrected and shipped back to Haiti. The large international fabric companies contract with an individual in Haiti to organize a sweat shop, and they supply them with old half worn out sewing machines, and advance them money to rent a building, The nation's leaders receive their fees for permits and other so-called grants, and bribes.

Then the International Money Fund is enticed to make a loan to this poor starving country, and the money of course winds up in the hands of the dictators, who are told they must be more austere in their management of their economy. As a result the dictators, and their henchmen tell the contractors in the sweat shops that they must pay their workers more or they would be closed down. The contractors are in competition with other sweat shop owners who contract with other companies of other nations. If they can't compete they close and the workers are again unemployed.

Why doesn't Congress have the decency to tell us the truth, knowing that they sold out to big business, who are the movers and shakers behind all trade issues.

The so-called human rights committee that is to be the watchdog is pure deceit on the part of the Congressmen. It was added simply to cover their backsides. They have no legal right, no moral authority and no ability to interfere with the internal affairs of China or any other sovereign state.

World trade is complex, bloated with intrigue. There are no easy answers, but rather than become enmeshed in the machinations of the deceit of tried and true nations of deceit, why can't this nation pull back, slow down, and examine what we have, instead of looking over the fence at supposedly greener pastures, and become clean and lean, instead of lean and mean. Why can't our multinational corporations set the example of the American Way to the world, instead of becoming one of them? Why can't our multinational corporations become more humanized and less politicized, and greedy.

We must always be alert when the government and industry become too enamored with one another.

Item # 9 Refers to Open Borders Immigration

The Statue of Liberty stands in the harbor of New York as a symbol of the spirit of America of yesteryear. Give me your poor, and oppressed, meant what it said, and the poor and the oppressed did come to America. The poor were offered an opportunity, and that was all, because that was all that this country had to offer. However the poor gave up family, homeland, and their roots just for an opportunity to live free, and have an opportunity to have food for themselves and family. The afflicted, the oppressed came to be free of tyranny, free from fear of torture of one kind or another for even being suspected of not agreeing with the king, or the tin-horn dictator.

These people built America. They were clean and lean, and if they weren't they were returned to their homeland. They took risks that we of today would shrink from, or would ask the government to guarantee our success.

These people came from around the world. When they arrived they of course sought out others of their culture simply because they could not speak English, and needed someone to help them until they could get started working. They did work under the most brutal conditions, many times in the sweat shops of the big cities until they could move on. They moved out into the wilderness, felled trees, and pulled up the roots with the help of a mule, and if they didn't have a mule they chopped them out in order to establish farmlands.

These people did form communities of people of their original nationality. They settled states, for example the Germans settled in Pennsylvania, and even in the cities they sought their own, such as what is now known as Germantown in Philadelphia. However of all of the different nationalities none called themselves German-Americans, or Irish-American, or Russian-American, they became Americans and helped build this great nation.

Today with our country's Open Border Policy swarms of people come to this nation from around the world to live the good life. They come to enjoy the fruits of those who labored before them. They come and complain that they must speak English in order to get a job, or because it is more difficult for their children in school. They expect all of the benefits of the American society without having anything to do with contributing to the system.

It is commonly known that the farmers on the West Coast could not harvest their crops without the use of imported labor. These laborers are to be checked and rechecked so that they do not became assimilated in the work force of America. They are given green cards to identify themselves. They are here for the picking season only, but they soon see the good life of America, the government benefits etc., and so they now plan to stay. They are told that if they apply for citizenship they can then become a citizen. They go to the local politician who tells them that if they vote the right way he will help them to become naturalized. Laws have been passed making it easier for these imported field workers to become citizens, or even allowing them to vote during the process.

The immigration act of 1990 raised the number of immigrants entering the country annually to 700,000, excluding refugees whose admission numbers are announced annually.

In 1998 9.3% of our total population or 25,000,000 were foreign born, and 7,000,000 have come from Mexico. Our lenient laws governing immigration are providing votes to the legislators who introduced and passed these laws.

In 1988 nearly 1,400.000 illegal aliens applied for amnesty under a new Federal Policy.

Taking into consideration the need for field workers on the West Coast, and the lobbying efforts of the huge farm combines it is reasonable to assume that the government and the combines get along pretty well.

Add to this, the number of illegal immigrants who invade our borders daily and it appears obvious that something is seriously wrong with our immigration policy

Why should people who are not starving, who are not being threatened physically be permitted to immigrate to this country? This nation cannot in any way give succor to all people of the world, if one considers just the continent of Africa with its sick and dying populations, brought about by the leaders of the people. Why should this nation distribute the hard earned benefits earned by the citizens of this country to those who just want to live better than they are in their own country.

The inflow of cheap labor reduces the living standard for the American worker.

Let our nation remain the hope of those who are truly hungry, and threatened by tyranny, and not be the Charlie Brown of the world.

With the radicals in Mexico shouting that one day they will take back the Southwest that belonged to them, and the Muslims wanting a state to call their own in this country, and with the black leaders demanding forty acres and a mule for every black family to compensate for their abuses over a hundred years ago, it is time to get serious about immigration.

Item # 10 Refers to More Centralized Government

Once the people of a nation forget that the troubles of that nation or any nation are the result of human nature, they will begin witnessing the loss of their freedoms. Let us always remember that we are all human, and are potential predators.

Years ago a T.V. program called the Shadow, used the quip; Who knows what evil lurks in the hearts of men? Then the answer is given' "The Shadow knows". Today we do not have the Shadow to give us the answer, we have it within ourselves.

Human nature is devious, dubious, and downright evil at times, as well as being kind and caring. It is the kind and caring part of human nature that the nation should be most concerned about. It is the kind and caring part of human nature that lulls the citizens to sleep. The question must be asked why anyone or any organization be concerned with my individual welfare. This question is asked in spite of the fact that there are many hundreds or possibly thousands of sincere individuals who give their lives caring for others, seeking no reward, or recognition, they find the reward within themselves. They live truth.

There is no question that many persons who enter politics do so with the sincere intention of making the world a better place in which to live. However if they remain in politics, human nature's dark side begins to raise its ugly head, and it is almost impossible to subdue the temptations, just as it almost impossible to subdue the evil temptations that we all experience.

Of all the people who have lived, are living, and will live in the future have or will experience evil temptations from time to time. Some who have learned the facts of truth can find a way to overcome, and the rest will be consumed by these evil temptations.

Why then should the people of any nation expect politicians to be any different? They are all human, with all of their good and bad traits. The problem lies in the tendency of human nature to follow the leader, the leader who may have charisma, who is assertive, and especially if the leader promises to care for the people, and makes demagogic speeches frightening the people to the point that they hate everyone except the leader. This type of leader desires more than life itself the adoration of the unthinking masses.

It is obvious that over the past sixty years the Federal government has insidiously infiltrated itself more and more into the lives of private citizens, either directly or indirectly.

There is not one piece of legislation that is passed that establishes as a legal right, a benefit, insured by the use of force that does not infringe upon the rights of others, and diminishes the others freedom.

It is also obvious that the politicians have constantly attempted to bypass the Constitution and the established laws in order to get what they want.

Back in the thirties, President Roosevelt twisted arms in any way he could to add another four or five judges to the Supreme Court in order to get his legislation enacted. He referred to the nine judges who sat at that time as old fogies who were not with the program, which meant of course, his programs.

President Roosevelt was a man of the hour, he was a great leader with vision. He had the ability to arouse hope in the people of America at a time when there was little or no hope, he was generally loved by the people of the country, who looked upon him as a father figure. He was innovative, he was strong, and he fought ferociously to get his visions passed into law, for the people.

However the Federal Savings and Loan industry, with its guarantee to the depositor that his deposit was insured by the Federal Government, was one of President Roosevelt projects. This was done to encourage people to again deposit their savings into a bank after years of bank bankruptcy. This plan with good intent meant that all taxpayers became liable to pay for the mismanagement of the banks insured, and pay they did when the Federal Savings and Loan Associations folded up like wet paper bags due to mismanagement, and fraud during the eighties, amounting to about three hundred billion dollars. This meant that the government could invade the private sector and extract taxes at will. President Roosevelt had the vision to see this possibility, and so stated. However it proves that regardless of the good intent and motive, encroachment had begun. Volumes could be written about this debacle of good intent. This did encourage home buying for the average person, where before they could not meet the terms of the mortgagor. Amortization of the mortgage spurred construction, and provided employment which was sorely needed at that time.

Social Security was a brainchild of President Roosevelt. It was of course initiated to give the elderly some sense of security when they could no longer support themselves, those who were laid off at the end of 25 or 30 years of service and received a gold watch in appreciation for their loyalty.

This is another good idea with good intent that permits the government by force of law to invade the private domain and extract taxes from citizens to support others not of their own family. Regardless of the blessings of this program who can deny that by far the majority of the recipients receive far more in benefits than they have paid in monthly premiums. Who pays the difference? The law makers of both parties have used this program to borrow off budget money to spend to secure votes.

The young are forced to pay the support for the elderly which they resent. This program of good intent has been used by our lawmakers since the great depression, to feather their nests by expanding the program to include many benefits never intended in the beginning. This issue is a vote getter.

In the sixties President Lyndon Johnson's Great Society Program initiated the Medicare program. Again this endeavor was one of good intent, and has been a blessing to millions of citizens providing them with the most basic needs, and permitting them to retain some semblance of self respect by charging them a monthly premium.

Again however from this program came the Medicaid program for the very poor, who are not receiving Medicare benefits, and cannot purchase private hospital and health insurance. Again the politicians have feathered their own nests by demagoguing both Social Security and Medicare, frightening the recipients of both, and those who hope to someday receive the benefits they are paying for today. The Social Security fund has been drained dry and an I.O.U. deposited to balance the books, and the benefits have been paid from the general funds for years. This fraudulent mismanagement of this huge monetary fund has been revealed recently by a few statesmen who could no longer stand by, and see the American public deceived. This deceit has now become prohibited, the Social Security Fund is now out of reach of the rank and file politicians.

As afore stated, the Social Security program, the Medicare program, and the Medicaid program have been and are a blessing to so many, in spite of fraud, and mismanagement. However lest we forget, these programs are costly in dollars, and have to be paid for in taxes, which are an infringement on our freedom Taxes are a relentless taskmaster, to the point that they become at times so oppressive as to ignite a national revolution.

If we now consider the multitudinous benefits that our benevolent government has bestowed upon us as gifts, labeled free of charge we can soon see the entrapment of the nation in the web of taxes alone.

As an example, the law requiring employers to guarantee a woman a job after childbirth absence seems like such a humane thing to do. However no one thinks of the cost to the employer in having to train another person to learn the requirements of the position. This cost of course must be added to the price of the goods or services sold to the consumer, which of course means the purchaser, or the taxpayer. Now the pressure is being applied to even pay the woman for her time away from her job.

Our government has pledged to put an additional 100,000 policemen on duty throughout the nation, with our government paying part of the cost.

Our government has provided us with thousands of volunteers to work throughout the nation providing the volunteers with a salary and expenses. Paid-Volunteers? Is this related to an oxymoron?

Add to this the telephone excise tax that the citizens have been paying for years with no explanation for the tax. The money was used for pet political projects to get votes.

The above are only a minuscule part of the whole, and our people have absorbed the cost through taxes, although our political leaders have presented them as gifts to the unthinking masses, especially around election time.

Government outlays, which include federal, state, local, and regulatory costs largely imposed on the private sector have grown more than 50% faster than the economy for 50 years, and now claims more than one third of the GDP. The federal government owns one-third of all land, pays for 40% of all medical care, manages nearly 50% of all retirement funds, and regulates many industries. Americans live and work in a web of government rules.

Our federal government is now engaged in open warfare with the tobacco industry. It is threatening lawsuits, and encourages lawsuits against the industry. This is a two-faced thrust in that on one side it sues the industry or threatens to sue, and demands that its advertising be changed, and on the other side it taxes the industry with exorbitant taxes to fill its coffers.

It would be safe to say that the use of tobacco is stupid, along with being harmful to the body and mind. It is mind altering in that it creates an addictive state to the point that the smoker is made a slave to the habit. When questioned before an investigative committee of the government regarding the addictive effects of smoking tobacco, the C.E.O..s of the industry all lied. Not one has ever been brought to trial on a charge of perjury. Why is this so? Could it be that the government does not want to kill the geese that are laying golden eggs? No morals here, just money for our leaders Just more solids in the cesspool. Our government is prosecuting a legitimate business, a legal business. If the tobacco industry is selling a product that is, as the government claims it is, harmful to the people, why doesn't the government close the industry down? The hypocrisy is quite obvious, when they won't legalize drugs such as crack, but legalize tobacco. Tobacco kills more slowly, it is not so romantic or dramatic, as is smoking crack, and there are apparently fewer politicians involved in the tobacco industry as in the crack industry.

First it was the telephone industry, then the tobacco industry, now it is the gun industry, and the computer industry. Where will our government stop spreading its tentacles into private and public affairs of men? Is the brewing industry next? What a source of taxation this industry is. The government won't close it down, it will just bleed it to death.

Morals cannot be legislated and industry cannot be made more humane by enacting laws. However anti-trust laws are a must to keep our industries from getting a strangle hold over the consumer.

Back in the so-called good ole days John D. Rockefeller who founded the Standard Oil company, would invade a town or a city and cut prices on petroleum products to the point where the competition would be forced out of business. Then he would raise the prices, and he alone decided how high to raise them, and the consumer had no redress or anywhere to go. This was the beginning of the anti-trust saga.

Our politicians appear to have no real concern for real reprisal from their constituents in light of the 1996 political fund-raising rampage. It appears that they are quite convinced that the American people are sufficiently dumbed down.

There must, from the attitude and actions taken by our leaders today, be a constant fantasy that one day they will wake up and find that there is no longer a constitution, or any of the three branches of government to restrict them in any way, then they all can be little despots running the government their way plundering power wherever they dare.

Fellow Americans, we have a new executive state that is expanding through extortion, and our fight for a limited government is fast becoming a losing battle. It is no longer just a battle, it is a war that is being lost. Let us all pray that we do not witness another depression. We no longer as a people have a foundation upon which to rebuild, the tried and true foundation has been deliberately pulverized.

Our government is not limited in scope, it is also not limited by the politics of legislatures. Increasingly our government is not limited by the rule of law, understood, perhaps quaintly, as power controlled by laws enacted by Congress. Our congress is complicit in all this because congress could stop it. If congress does not stop it this nation will experience what one has named; a strip mall socialism, with sprawling government, ubiquitous, and undistinguished , with no theme or theory, just momentum. Momentum, fast movement to where?

This is not alarmist rhetoric, it has happened and is happening. Our nation is heading for a breakup, and there is no longer any established authority that can stop it, only the people rising up and demanding that our politicians in congress develop a backbone and a sense of decency, and legislate for the general welfare of the people, and not for themselves, and the little serfdom of their little districts.

The cleaning of the cesspool which represents the government of the United States of America will be done by the voters at the ballot box or by the mobs in the streets led by a charismatic leader. It is still our choice.

A Contradictive Comparison "Tradition"

What is tradition? Originally it meant to deliver. The handing down orally of beliefs, customs, stories etc. from one generation to another. Any long established custom, or practice handed down. What was handed down from the people themselves is a far cry from what we have today. Granted, customs change. They change for many reasons. Again however the changes in custom should never be made if those changes are going to demand that the foundation of right or wrong, decency, respect for others, are imperiled, because that leaves one with nothing but a change in custom, and possibly a few more toys to play with.

The founding fathers of this nation, realizing that customs change and stories lengthened and shortened, added to and subtracted from did not leave their beliefs that they sacrificed so much for to the whims of memory alone. They wrote out in quite detail the Constitution of the nation, along with the Bill of Rights.

It may have been better if they never wrote the Bill of Rights. These rights are now being interpreted to mean whatever a perpetrator with distorted visions wants them to mean. For example the First Amendment is used to justify a person to place a cross into a bottle, and then urinate into the bottle, and describe this act as art. Or the Virgin Mary and child created out of cow dung, and then praised as an expression of art. Or the burning of the flag of the nation as expression.

The traditional American consensus was for the most part a contradiction of the Establishment positions. The Traditional American consensus was;

1 Christianity

Founded upon an expectation that the government would reflect Christian morality, America is today a post Christian nation, governed by the secular Establishment, with an unrelenting force from all directions to eradicate it entirely.

Secular humanism is deemed to be the new religion. It promotes ethical relativism, and regards traditional institutions to be outdated and in need of overhaul or eradication

Yes, Christians can still read their Bible, and have open Bible study meetings, but Christianity is no longer the culture refining religion it once was due in part to Christians who talk the talk but will no longer walk the walk.

America is not so far along the road of humanism that it can't find its way home, and by home, it is meant returning to our Christian roots. This cannot happen and will not happen until Christians stop reading about the Bible, and read the Bible.

Only one generation after the publishing of " The Humanist Manifesto", abortion is a multi-million dollar industry, promiscuity is encouraged, "Values" are ridiculed, Laws often protect the guilty rather than the victim. Patriotism is giving away to globalism.

Secular humanism will only succeed in wooing America away from its roots to the degree that it has nowhere else more relevant and helpful to turn. Offer something better, more real, to take its place, and it doesn't stand a snowball's chance in Hades.

Please ask yourself this question. What is America today?

2

The nation's tradition valued human life and strongly disapproved of abortion.

3

Our tradition encouraged trade and commerce, but it was to remain aloof from the rest of the world's quarrels and wars. It sought to avoid entangling alliances.

4

Our tradition views homosexuality as an aberration, and from the biblical view, a sin.

5

Our tradition favored a hard- money system and opposed legal tender laws that compel people to accept government-issued currency.

6

Our tradition favors an aristocracy of merit while insisting that government must be neutral and neither reward nor punish any group of citizens based on politics, race, gender or ethnic origin.

7

Our tradition seeks racial harmony while conceding that a total elimination of racial prejudice, on both sides, is probably impossible.

8

Our tradition favored an "American First " approach to trade and foreign relations and believed that raising the American standard of living should be the goal of all trade policies

9

Our tradition sees the nation-state as the best form of government possible and jealously guards the nation's independence.

10

Our tradition always wanted a tightly controlled immigration policy, admitting only those who can make a positive contribution to America.

11

Our tradition favors dispersing the powers of government to provide checks and balances and to limit those powers severely

Note

The above eleven items were contributed by Charley Reese, columnist for the Orlando Sentinel.

THE UNFATHOMABLE MYSTERY?

In the scriptures we find the question; "Why do the heathen rage?" Who are the heathen? The heathen are those who seek the maximum of the hedonistic life. The heathen are those who are not enlightened, the sole makers of themselves, they have much knowledge but very little if any wisdom. They are driven by the forces of the world. They are always attempting to prove their worth by succeeding according to the rules of what other people think of them. They are usually strongly opinionated, and must have their own way because they never appear to reach maturity. To them the end usually justifies the means, and a little fraud or deceit is mixed into the batter to accomplish what in their minds must be accomplished if they expect to reach the level of success that will bring the praise of men.

They claim to be individualists, but they are in realty very much dependent upon the acclaim of the world.

They tell the world of their long term planning for business increase, but in reality they see very little other than what they want to see. They will not face reality, they will not face the truth, all the while wringing their hands about the conditions surrounding them. If forced to face the truth they will become angry and begin hurling names against the wind, and blame others for their despair.

The above refers not only to so many business people, but unfortunately to the rank and file, the average citizen, and that is the calamity, because it is the average citizen who feels the brunt of the zealots. The radical fringe has infiltrated the minds of the citizens of this nation to the point where they are not sure of the difference between right and wrong regarding so many things, and especially those things that effect their present individual lives.

The baby boomer generation, and their children are living in a dream world. They are living a purposeless life except a constant seeking for more fun. They feel empty, unsatisfied, and anxious. They refuse to reason, and will not even consider anything other than their opinion even if it means that they will continue with their heavy burden forever. They are in a state of derision, and have no idea as to where to go to lighten their burden, except to a counselor, and even then they will not listen, if what is said is contrary to what they think.

They listen to the talking heads on T.V. who are becoming wealthy spieling their psychobabble to these people in the pain of their own making. These heathens are hypocrites, as they complain but will under no conditions even consider the possibility of a change in attitude or thinking.

Why is this chapter entitled; The "Unfathomable Mystery"?, followed by a question mark? There are two main reasons for this title. One is that the problems such as school shootings, drug addiction. racial tensions, crime, the steady decline in wholesome homes, etc. are considered a mystery when there is no mystery. These subjects are talked to death with no results.

Another reason is that the author who is doing quite well at present doesn't like what he sees coming in the near future for himself or his posterity. He considers it a pity to see such a wonderful experiment such as our democracy being suffocated by the heathen, the rebels without a cause continuing to rip apart the delicate fabric of our constitutional government.

They do this with no real intent to destroy, but as what has been said of old; "the road to hell is paved with good intentions." "The devil is in the detail", and the majority of the heathen do not have the common sense to stop, reason and begin to see the ramifications of their demands.

There never has been, and there is not now, or will there ever be perfection in our government, because the politicians are human, and there never was, there are none now, nor will there ever be a perfect human being. Does this mean that we should all live without hope? Of course not, but in order to live with one another in this life, we must establish a civilization of law, not men, regulations backed by force simply for individual and personal safety.

Humanity has climbed up out of the dark ages to some degree, but the causes for the dark ages are deep within us as humans. We are naturally predators. We can acquire much knowledge but we must seek and find wisdom, else we perish. We can do this best in a country where the individual can feel free to express and do. This country was The United States of America until the light was dimmed by double speak, hypocrisy, political correctness, and career politicians who are human. We have become a nation of humanists, and the Humanist Manifesto is now being accepted by more and more citizens of this country. Christianity is being slowly but surely cast aside like an old shoe, or a worn out dishcloth.

The hedonistic urge is upon us, and growing stronger especially now during this time of plenty. Things instead of spirit, things instead of soul, things instead of decency, things instead of caring, things instead of sharing, things instead of true living, things instead of children, things instead of home, things instead of human relations, things instead of country, things instead of God, and it will be things that will tear us apart.

The need for wisdom is so great, yet so plentiful, but so few who seek it, and fewer who persevere and find it. It has always been those who have found it that have given some light to the materialistic world and kept it from destroying itself, those who sincerely care and were considered by their fellow men as fools for not seeking only material riches. "What can one give in exchange for his or her soul? When the concern for the soul diminishes, life becomes cheap and meaningless.

When communications are diminished, problems evolve, people are separated one from another, more time is spent alone, and no lasting relationship developed, hence lonesomeness is the result, and a feeling of not belonging.

The media as a whole has had a hey day covering the school shootings. These shootings are dramatic, and for some reason they appear to be relished by the general public, they appear to hit a mourning note in people, like going to a funeral. The people say how horrible, then ask the question; Why? The talking heads in the newspapers, and on T.V. spend hours talking about it, and the theorists, the child psychologists, and the experts give a liberal dose of their idea as to how, and why this happens, and they offer their thoughts free. What these people suggest might work on an individual basis but not as a cure -all to a national problem.

What works on an individual basis is generally temporary, because when the counseling is over the individual must have something to build a life on, a rock foundation, if they do not have this foundation they will most assuredly revert back to their old habits of thinking, and it is a matter of thinking.

There have always been and there will always be those who are considered aberrations from the accepted norm. What is being considered here is not just an aberration, what is being considered here has to do with personal suffering, for the perpetrator, his or her family, and friends, as well as the victim's family. What is being considered here is an epidemic of a disease of the mind that is destroying the nation as a whole while the citizens go about wringing their hands crying why, what can we do? However if they were shown the answer, and that answer required a change in thinking and attitude they would ridicule it.

Considering the above, let us just for a moment picture the next to perfect scenario. We see a home not only a house. The home we see is mortgaged, it is furnished warmly, but modestly, paid for in full. The furniture was paid for before the marriage. There are two automobiles, one a station wagon about four years old, and the other a three year old Toyota which the father uses to go to work and back home. Both of the cars are of course paid for in full. The father's income is $40,000 annually The wife's salary was $30,000 annually. The mother, father and children are warmly dressed, they look neat, and clean, but none of the clothing is of a designer make. The mother and father have set up a budget to guide their spending.

Included in the budget is house repair, car repair, clothing, vacations, children's education, and retirement.

The family attend church on a regular basis, with the children attending bible studies, all realizing that they must be fed spiritual food for a healthy spiritual life, again realizing that without a spiritual life, they would be as empty shells, seeking insatiable pleasure only in material things.

Only one credit card company is used, the husband and wife each having a card. They do not have a card for each department store, or oil company. This allows them to see how much money they are spending, for what, and how often.

This is quite a responsibility for any man to bear, but bear it he will if he is a man who loves his wife and children. He accepts the challenge and is proud. He did not enter into this marriage frivolously, on a trial basis.

The mother has a bachelor degree, and was teaching school until her first child was born. She being an adult made the decision to stay home full time to be there for the children. She realized that to do so she would be in a sense, shut in with all of the mundane, repetitive duties that never seem to end, a seemingly thankless task with no end for years to come.

The three children were normal and confident, knowing who they were. They often inquired why they could not have designer sneakers with lights on the heels, and why dad didn't buy a new car every two years like their friends' dads did etc. The standard answer from both mother and dad was; We cannot afford it at this time. When the two girls came home with eyes swollen from crying, because they were not invited to a certain function, or a boy appeared to notice other girls more than them, mother was there to listen, hug, and explain away their hurts.

When the son came home one night and told his father that his close friend's father bought him a car, and asked why he didn't buy him one, the father told him that he could not afford it and that if the son wanted to buy a car he could work and earn enough to buy one and pay for the upkeep, but that he loved him and was there for him. The son was quite upset, so he got a job bagging groceries at a large super market. He did buy a car and kept it up, and later told his many friends what a lesson he had learned through that experience. He later became a millionaire, because he had learned that he could have whatever he wanted if he was willing to work for it.

This family experienced all of the unexpected problems that all people, and all families experience, but they had a love and respect for one another that pulled them through the rough spots.

They could do this because they did not have the unbearable weight of buying beyond their means, trying to live other people's lives, with a half dozen credit cards charged to the limit. They did not attempt to do two jobs in order to live up to the Jones. Neither parent came home at night dead tired, and then have to cook dinner, and wash the dishes, wash the clothes, put the children to bed, and lay out clothes for the morrow. They could rest and spend time with family, supervising homework, converse about the events of the day, creating lasting memories of home and hearth.

Above all, mother or dad were there for the children, and the children knew they belonged.

This family would be classified as a typical traditional family with family values, but a dull boring experience by the all knowing, the hip, the with it scatter brains, who are living in big circles, going round and round going nowhere wondering what it is all about. They feel empty and have no idea what to do or where to go to find solid fulfilling direction for their lives. They are the ones who ask why these school shootings occur and haven't the slightest idea as to how to stop them.

Why do the heathen rage, and why are the people in derision?

With big business pushing for sales, and the government pushing for consumer spending to keep the economy running at top speed for political purposes, and the American public addicted to consumerism, should there be any question as to why there is little or no stability in the lives of so many, especially the young people who are our posterity.

In order to present the scenario more vividly let us consider a typical family of four, a husband and wife, with two children living in their suburban wonderland. The husband earns $ 40,000 per year, and the wife earns $ 30,000 annually. They bought a $250,000 house with four bedrooms, with four bathrooms. The building lot is beautifully landscaped, with a swimming pool at the back of the house. They had only one bedroom furnished at the time of their marriage, along with a small table in the kitchen with four chairs. They decided to go ahead and furnish the entire house on credit, and pay a little per month for it, which of course means interest payments, money spent for which there is no tangible return.

Separate from the house is a two car garage. Both parents work to support their lifestyle, so they both have relatively new cars, which they trade every two to three years, on a three to five year payment plan, which again includes interest payments.

With both parents working, and with two children, a clothing account soon accumulates which is covered with a credit card allowing for minimum payments. Living in a new exclusive subdivision requires dressing in sync with one's neighbors, but with a credit card with all major department stores, and practically every oil company, and banks, these things are taken care of.

This couple sincerely want to be good parents, and they believe that what they are doing is for the children as well as themselves. They both came from modest homes living with parents who struggled all their lives to maintain a home, who spent a lifetime acquiring a household of furniture, who could afford only one car for dad to take him to his job and back. They were loved and mother was there for them, but they wanted much more for their children and themselves, and they wanted it now. The interest they were paying was close to the salary their dads earned per year.

These parents were conscious of the necessity for a good education for their children, so they set up a plan combining life insurance with government bonds to pay tuition and board for the children when they finished secondary school. The employers of both parents participated in a 401-k plan for the parents retirement, which of course is in a sense a forced savings, and a drain on the cash flow. The employer also carried a health-care plan for both. This couple lived about 20 miles from a huge lake. For recreation on the weekends, the family would go to the lake, sometimes for the weekend. It wasn't long before the boat fever overcame them, so they decided to buy a boat because it would be so much fun for the kids.

With so many other pressing places for their cash, and having no reserve cash, they decided to take out a second mortgage on their house. They were told that the lending company would lend them up to 125% of the value of their house, minus the amount of the balance of their first mortgage, because their credit was so good. They decided to borrow the limit because they could then pay for the boat on a monthly pay plan, and have a little reserve to put into the bank giving them a 1% return on their deposit while they are paying the second mortgage company 11% interest on the loan.

After about a year the boat became mundane, and they decided to learn scuba diving. They finished the lessons and then bought gear. Then they could use the boat to take them anywhere on the lake in search of hidden treasure.

What a happy picture of a happy family being together with their children.

In the mean time the children are getting older and grown up. They are going to school and having the usual problems of being accepted, or scorned in their young minds. They had heartbreaks in their love lives, and felt that they were not equal in beauty, humor, intelligence, personality, or the teacher just didn't like them. They cried in their souls, but there was no where to go, because mother and dad were both working long hours to keep up with their obligations. They had become slaves to the money lenders. The money lenders were ruthless. When the debtor was a little late in making his or her monthly payment, they would find out where the debtor was at anytime of the day and call them, regardless of the embarrassment to the debtor.

The family did not attend church because they could not understand how God could give them more than they already had. They had accumulated all these things without His help, and they were certain that they were not any more of a sinner than anyone else. They just couldn't go along with this being saved business. Unfortunately they did not understand that church not only promises salvation, but also teaches one wisdom which teaches one the principles by which to live. It teaches one who they are, it teaches one to discern, it teaches one self reliance, it teaches one not to try to live someone else's life, and not seek approval from anyone, because you are confident that knowing who you are, and where you are going does not depend upon the opinion, nor is it the business of other people. You are an individual. The church teaches that love is the most powerful force in the universe, not the sword. Love drives out fear, and the truth of love sets one free from trying to live a life based on the approval of others.

To sum up, the children never had a mother or father to come home to, when they were babies they were dropped off at a day care center, nurtured by hard working people who had many children to care for. These were and are people who in most cases work for the minimum wage with little education or vocabulary. The more one knows the easier it is to learn, Children learn from those who nurture them and surround them.

These children grow up, and attend primary, and secondary school and these are the years that they are left strictly on their own, with no one to turn to. The parents are working so hard for things. When their children want a pair of designer sneakers they buy them on the card. Later when they want a car, they buy them one, and charge it. No one can say that these parents ever deprived their children of anything, they loved their children very much! Did they, or were they doing what they wanted to do to look good, and gain the approval of their neighbors, and relatives because they did not have the backbone to live their own lives?

With all of their things the children were still alone whether in the urban area or the suburban area, and this lonesomeness is the breeding ground for the school shooters, the crime sprees, the promiscuity, the drug addiction, and the inability to love. These are not bad kids, they are lonesome kids, and without the close parental guidance they will join the groups suffering from the same affliction. The peer pressure to experiment is always with them. In spite of what the parents have told them, in a weak moment of wanting to belong to something, they will slip and fall. The next time it will be easy, because they now have the excitement, and the sense of belonging.

There will always be school shooters. crime sprees, promiscuity, drug addiction, but these things will be the life style of those who are generally aberrations from the norm of a healthy civilization. The subject at hand is not the aberrations of a few, but the epidemic of this life style which is engulfing the nation and being accepted as the norm. It is being accepted as the norm because the citizens of the nation have accepted it and because they have no idea as to what they can do about it. This is the crime against children, and the nation.

This issue, this topic, has been talked to death by the experts, the talking heads, and politicians on T.V , but the epidemic is widening, and will continue to widen until something is done about it. The big question is; what to do. The solution is very simple, but it is not easy, because it will require a change in thinking, a change in attitude, and a change for many in life style.

It will require mothers to stay home and be there for their children, regardless of the fact that they will not have all of the things of the Jones's, but they will be better mothers and women. It will require Dad to assume the responsibility for providing and protecting his family, making him truly a better man.

In by far the majority of cases, families will have to change their life styles, and have less of the material things, smaller houses, smaller and older cars, maybe no boats, or airplanes, only more time to spend with their children. They will live within their means, and not on credit cards bought out to the hilt, or second mortgages with high interest rates. They will at last be free from the slavemaster; credit. They can then plan to establish a more suitable life style after their feet are on solid ground. They can think more clearly, after they have shed the monster; strain, and become free men and women again raising their children in an atmosphere of security instead of one of constant crisis. They can feel the joy of being individuals developing an inner strength they never knew they had.

The children must be number one priority, number two will not do. God first, then the wife, children and husband. Excuses will not do, such as; we are doing it for our children even if we do not have time to love them.

Let us face the truth! How many of today's baby boomers, and their children will have the intestinal fortitude to change their thinking, their attitudes, their life styles to create a more healthy world for their children? Answer: very few.

This generation of parents will continue to commit the crime against their children, they will sacrifice their children on the altar of things in the name of; we are doing all this for our children.

Let us stop talking and do something about it. If we are not going to do anything about it, then please let us stop talking about it, and covering it up by talking about gun control, and other drivel.

In regard to the above, let us be reminded that this economy is consumer driven, which means that the consumers are keeping the boom alive. The billions in tax increases by President Bush, and then many more billions in tax increases by President Clinton, along with the new technology industry growing on venture capital, thereby avoiding bank borrowing, has created the greatest sustained economic boom in history. It is a bought economy. It has been bought with taxpayer's money, and can be brought to a halt when the taxpayer decides that he or she is working to pay taxes.

Should the people in the second scenario above decide to give their children love instead of things, and this occurred instantaneously, the economy would collapse over night. The chances of this happening is moot, because it would require that these parents would gain instant wisdom which would require their changing their thinking, and attitude overnight.

All we can hope and pray for is that the pendulum begin to slow down in its present direction, and eventually begin in the opposite direction.

The one problem that is at the root of the shootings, drug addiction, promiscuity etc., is the accepting of immorality. Not bad people, but just hedonistic heathen who are living in derision, wondering what is happening about them, seeking answers in strange places.

CHURCH AND STATE

This chapter is in a sense, a book within a book. It is the essence of the reason that this book was written. The issue of the separation of the church and state has divided this nation's people, and is slowly but surely changing the complexion, the personality, the culture of the country, because it is weakening the strong heart of the nation.

Why does one write about this subject, when the writer knows that few will read it, and of the few only a few will take it to heart and reason about it? Because this is a pleading to stop, look, and listen before crossing over the line of no return. We have allowed prosperity to enslave us. Instead of gratitude we are becoming more demanding of things. Our souls is shrinking.

There is no suggestion here that the reader follow the guide lines of the writer's opinion, or that the reader begin to live the life of the writer, but the reader is beseeched to at least consider the thought that is not new, but must be reasoned with, for the good of us all. Truth is the most powerful force in the world, and few there are who find it. Truth is always moving through all of the man made misery, and deprivation, on its way to victory. Whether the victory is soon or late is up to society, and no one else. When truth triumphs, the cornucopia of the earth's plenty will become a blessing instead of the reason for man's inhumanity to man.

It appears as though the subject of church and state is no longer a question of separating all things pertaining to the church, from all things pertaining to the state, but there now appears to be an insidious force, a power, a well organized entity with apparent influence in high places whose aim is to eradicate religion from the borders of America.

To some this may have a paranoid ring, but the Soviet Union did in its heyday decree that in order to bring another nation into their orb, it was first necessary to confuse the religions, and the message of the church.

The citizens of America have been pressured to accept that the Constitution of the U.S. demands that any vague connection between the church and state be severed, and anything religiously associated, reserved only to the home, or the house of worship of a person's particular religion.

What hypocrisy. Every session of congress is opened with a prayer given by a chaplain, and our means of exchange still carries the words; "In God we trust".

Enough bantering. Let us get to the understanding of the enormity of the outcome of the decision of the Supreme Court. This court is, as everyone should know, established to interpret the Constitution. They are to interpret the intent of the writer, the spirit of the word, and the meaning of the word itself. The interpretations are not to be made based on any one of the justice's personal opinion, persuaded by any one justice's religious persuasion, and certainly not on political influence. Apparently this has happened, and is happening. The nation is being told daily how the outcome of the election of Nov. 2000 will effect the court. The effect of the election on the Supreme Court will resonate to the religious liberties of the people.

What exactly does the Constitution say about the matter of church and state? Under the heading of the Bill of rights, which consists of the first ten amendments, Amendment number one states, "Congress shall make no law respecting an establishment of religion, or prohibiting the free exercise thereof, or abridging the freedom of speech, or of the press, or the people peaceably to assemble, and to petition the Government for a redress of grievances".

It is quite clear to any reasonable person that the founding fathers wanted to avoid the tragic past of the state and the church sharing power. The state would hold the physical power and control and the church would hold the spiritual power and control over millions of souls. The people would find it impossible to escape the material misery imposed by the state at will, and the superstitious misery imposed by the so-called church, which threatened their very souls, if they did not obey the dictates of the state. For this we should thank our God for this inalienable right, and the wisdom of the founders of this great nation, the land of the free and the home of the brave.

Every citizen is protected by this amendment, whether it be attempted to be imposed by any village, town , county, state, or the Federal government.

How enticing it is for those of limited vision to declare that this is a Christian nation, and all should become Christians, or remain quiet. Like it or leave it. This is what the pilgrims and the citizens of Great Britain did, they left it, and formed a more perfect union. This country is composed of people of different nationalities, and they hold many different religious beliefs, which they hold near and dear to them. This is of course a common fact. They must be permitted, no, it is their inalienable right to worship according to conscience. Even the carpenter from Galilee, who didn't build a stairway leading nowhere, never demanded that anyone follow Him. He gave the people a choice. He pleaded that they come unto Him.

Congress shall make no law establishing religion, or prohibiting the exercise thereof.

It is obvious that no governmental entity shall ever establish a religion. On the other hand no governmental entity shall prohibit the free exercise of any religion. People of America can pray, meditate in prayer, anywhere, and in any place, without fear of governmental interference, or threat.

Therefore the citizens of this nation can if they so desire pray at baseball games, football games, soccer games etc. whether they be professional, or college activities.

However when the prayer session is organized, and a public address system is used, paid for by all taxpayers, when the land or the building used for this organized prayer session is paid for by all citizens, and when those attending these functions are of many different religious persuasions, and with so many of these learning institutions being subsidized and given grants for research by the Federal government, and with the administrators of these institutions giving their stamp of approval, the rights of those not affiliated with the popular religion of that institution are being abridged. This is unconstitutional.

Therefore no governmental entity shall in any manner even attempt to establish a national religion. However the same governmental entity must ensure the free expression of any individual religion.

This same government entity protects its citizens from religion. This is true freedom for all. All must be free, else none will be free for long. America, the land of the free, and the home of the brave. Yes, the home of the brave. It takes courage, it takes bravado at times to stand alone amidst the clamoring of the political correctors, and declare liberty, justice, freedom for all.

Lest we forget; some of the world's most horrible atrocities have been committed in the name of the Prince of Peace and Love, Jesus of Nazareth. Today the world is not suffering any shortage of religious zealots who would impose their empty ignorance upon the nation. The world is not suffering a shortage of non-religious zealots who would not hesitate a moment to impose their Humanist Manifesto that all that matters is knowledge, with their relative truths, that produces leaders like Joseph Stalin, Adolph Hitler, empty souls seeking the holy grail of power, where the end always justifies the means.

The world's people have suffered so much from the religious zealots, and the non- religious zealots. It is not now nor will it ever be easy to balance the two.

One's religious beliefs, and worship is or should be an extremely personal matter, between himself, or herself, and their God. It is not something you join, and then stand ready to do battle with all who are not of the same private club. Our religious beliefs determine who we are, what we are, and how we view the world in general.

It is utterly ridiculous to try to separate the church and the state, for as the religious thinking of the citizens go, so goes the government and the nation. It is a matter of choice, what do the people want?

Until the Declaration of Independence in America the people of the world chose to be shepherded by the Aristocrats, and the established church, and like sheep, they went before their shearers and opened not their mouths, and oh, how they were fleeced.

> Mind is the master power that molds and makes,
> and man is mind and evermore he takes,
> the tool of thought and shaping what he wills,
> brings forth a thousand joys or a thousand ills.
> He thinks in secret and it comes to pass,
> his environment is but his looking glass.

It is a matter of choice as to how our minds will be guided. Will they be guided by the temporal, the cheap, the gross, the crass seeking for material wealth, fame, or power, or will they be guided by the wisdom of the ages that offers a full life for all? The choice is ours now, will it be for evermore? There is not now nor should there ever be any compulsion which robs mankind of its inalienable rights of freedom. Even the right to remain stupid.

With all of our warts, what has made America the most influential, the wealthiest, the most generous, the leader of freedom in the world?

The answer to the above is that our constitution, the rock of our foundation of our government is based, has its roots, has its very being, and draws its strength from the principles of the Judeo-Christian doctrine of faith.

The Christian faith and religion is not just another faith or religion. It stands alone in the world as the enlightener, leading people from darkness into the wonderful light of wisdom, and the resurrection of the person from the death of shallow meandering for the tinseled nothingness, and exposes them to the real, the facts, the truth of life, leading to a life of material fulfillment with gratitude.

The principles upon which our constitution is laid are divine principles, revealed by the Creator to men who were given the strength to wager their lives and fortunes to implement these principles. However ours is not a Theocratic government. This type of conviction is a far cry from the general conviction of today, where men and women who declare themselves Christians, accept the diluted truth of political correctness espoused by so many churches, who do not want to be considered old fashioned, and endanger the membership rolls. The following is an analogy of the above thought, whether it be true or not is not known.

A squad of Russian soldiers marched into a church in a Russian village one Sunday morning and ordered the services halted. The leader told the priest to tell the members of the congregation, that all who would renounce their faith by walking out would be safe, and those who did not walk out would be shot.

The priest did what the leader commanded. Two thirds of the congregation walked out. One of the soldiers then closed the doors, and the entire squad sat down, and asked the priest to continue with his sermon.

After the service the priest told the leader of the squad that he did not understand the meaning of the soldiers' actions. The leader answered and said; " Father, we wanted to attend church and be fed the spirit of truth, but we didn't want to be surrounded by the weak in spirit, the faint of heart, the hypocrites.

Of course the cry will be heard that this story advocates radicalism, to be asked to accept death for a religious belief is absurd. Faith is to comfort you, not to cause tension, or be a threat.

It has been wisely said, that the pain of death is not in dying, but the pain of death is having never lived. If one does not have something that he or she is willing to die for, he or she has never really had anything to live for.

It has been written; "He who seeks to save his life shall lose it, but he who loses his life for my name's sake shall find it". A coward dies a thousand deaths, a courageous man but one. Only the spirit of truth firmly implanted in the soul gives this outlook on life.

One's religious faith or belief, or association with, is a very personal matter. It is an individual matter. It is between an individual, and his or her God.

It is surely a pity that the churches of today have become to at least some degree the pollster of the world, and like the political parties, they change their doctrine to satisfy the majority.

The truth is the truth, and nothing but the truth. It is uncompromisable. If it is diluted it becomes a harmful, and at times a deadly potent force for evil and harm to the masses. The church cannot be instructed by the world, it must instruct the world to lead it out of the abyss of its own making, which has caused so much unnecessary suffering. Yet the church seeks the approval of the world, only to find its membership rolls slipping every year.

There is becoming a severe shortage of pastors, and priests in the large denominational churches. In order to alleviate this condition, the large denominations are merging in order to fill one another's pulpits.

Below is an excerpt from Bishop John W. Howe of the Central Florida Diocese, after having just attended a General Convention; "General Convention is huge, unwieldy, intense, very expensive, complicated, confusing, and highly political. I always come away thinking there must be a better way to run a church."

Have they ever thought of searching the scriptures for answers to some of the knotty questions? If the scriptures do not give the answers to these questions, then the scriptures are not any more than the philosophical teachings along the lines of the ancient Greek writers.

A story is told of the very old retiring pastor of a rather small congregation in a small community. He was handing his mantle over to a young man who had just been ordained from a large denominational seminary. The congregation had been growing as the population had increased.

After about six months the young preacher wrote to the old preacher and told him of his concern that his congregation was stagnating. He explained that he had conducted parties, dances, dinners, and all kinds of activities, but to no avail. His congregation was not growing, in fact he believes it is shrinking. He asked if the old pastor could offer something helpful. The old preacher wrote back, with this question; "Have you tried preaching the Gospel?"

Back to Bishop John W. Howe. He further states in his article; " The other major issue that Convention had to deal with was Human Sexuality.

"About three weeks before we left for Denver the Presiding Bishop and the President of the House of Deputies decided to form a Special Committee to deal with the multitude of Resolutions that were coming in on the subject. Six bishops and six deputies, three clergy and three lay, were appointed by the respective Presidents, Bishop Greswold asked me to be one of the six bishops".

With such a gathering of talking heads as this there is no wonder the membership of the churches are shrinking, a perfect example of a loss in direction.

Again back to Bishop John W. Howe, as he goes further with his report; "At our get-acquainted session it was apparent we represented the full range of opinion on the subject of sexuality in general and homosexuality in particular. Three of our deputies were very openly "out" homosexual persons living in long-term committed relationships".

Further he states; "What you hope will happen with a committee such as ours is that it will craft some kind of a middle-ground. Resolution supported by at least a strong majority of its members. And if that is accepted by Convention, the committee then asks to be discharged from all other Resolutions. I honestly did think we could find such a middle ground".

The above report given by Bishop Howe is mentioned to simply present a picture of the confusion in just about all denominational churches today. This is not done to condemn or agree with the procedures of Convention.

What is objected to is the consensus sought is not on the scriptures upon which the church is guided, but on the opinion of the world, as presented by the representatives representing the membership.

It appears as though the church today is saying; We must please every-body, because if we don't we will lose membership, and we must give the impression that we are an inclusive organization.

There is nothing that can be presented to the world that will please every one.

The church came first which did the teaching. Then came the scrip-tures that reveal what the church taught. It is upon the scriptures that a consensus must be made, not a consensus of what the world thinks..

In regard to inclusiveness, the true church of the beginning is very inclusive. It casts out no one. It invites all to come to the knowledge of truth. The church is an organization of sinners.

To sum up; Is it possible to ask a simple question without inviting all the name calling, and the giving of labels such as fundamentalist, legalist, radical, or nut-cake? Is the Christian Church, which is described in scrip-ture as the ones called out, or the body of Christ, truly teaching what the scriptures reveals, or is it attempting to please everyone by accepting what the world thinks it wants, without structure or discipline

It is, unfortunately for the world, doing the latter, and as a result this nation and the world is sinking lower and lower into the abyss of degrada-tion, and emptiness.

As the religious thinking of the people goes, so goes the nation. It is impossible to separate the two. This is why the church must be revitalized by the renewing of the mind and not be conformed to the thinking of the world. We are not talking about my church or your church, we are talking about the universal church which is the body of Christ, the called out from every nation of the world. We should thank our God that there are still members of the body of Christ sitting in the pews of the very worldly churches of today.

The founding fathers of this nation were revitalized individuals, receiv-ing their revitalization from a revitalized church, which was liberated from the shackles of a state run church, and the people said "Amen". May we in this nation cast out the world run church, and return to the pristine beauty of the truth. The consensus of the nation in the beginning was the truth, and that the scriptures were divinely revealed, and with all of the opposing opinions regarding worldly activities being regarded as a part of human nature.

Political correctness has cowered the American people into believing that to voice one's strong religious persuasions is narrow minded, or even mean spirited, or even more incorrect to put these religious thoughts into print. This is the entity that is subtly, but surely smothering the truth in this nation.

Christianity teaches that; "God is Spirit, and those who worship Him must worship Him in Spirit and in Truth". We are not to worship Him in the name of Luther who did not want a church named after him, or Calvin, or the presbytery, or John the Baptist, or the Archbishop of Canterbury or the Pope or any other splinters broken off from the true church which is the embodiment of the Truth.

These denominations have in a sense served a good purpose, in that they offered the spirit filled individuals a sense of belonging, supporting one another in their battle against corruption in the so called church, and led in most cases by Spirit filled men, supported by Spirit filled women. Unfortunately these groups eventually took on the names of the individual leaders of reform, or were named after a specific verse in scripture.

And again unfortunately these groups became churches in their own names, and became adversaries toward one another, each claiming that only they have the truth, and you can find it nowhere else, all in the name of fighting for God. More atrocities have been committed in the name of God than in any other name, or reason.

The church is the called out Spirit filled individuals searching for truth.

Jesus taught; " I am the Way, the Truth, and the Life and no man comes to the Father, but by me". He teaches the Way, the Truth, and a life as it was meant to be from the beginning, filled with peace of mind, inner strength, principle, and freedom for the soul. He died to impress the message of truth into the minds of men and women. It is this message and His principles that founded America. The name of this source of wisdom is; "Traditional Christianity". It is a matter of choice, your choice, all are invited, no one is turned away.

Let us for a moment compare this nation with a few other nations, and see what makes them what they are.

Note; In regard to the below comparisons, GDP is used instead of GNP.

GDP equals the market value of all goods and services that have been bought for final use.

Per capita income equals the total income divided by the number of people in the group. They equate.

United Kingdom

Government; Constitutional Monarchy
GDP per capita; $21,200
Literacy Rate; 100%
Religion; Christian
Note; This is a Monarchy, with a class system.
Its church is state subsidized, post Christian.
Losing its influence in the world.

France

Government; Republic
GDP per capita; $22,700
Literacy Rate; 99%
Religion; Christian, Roman Catholic
Note; This is a republic, with socialistic leaning.

Russia

Government; Federal Republic
GDP; per capita, $4,700
Literacy Rate. 99%
Religion. Christian, Russian Orthodox, Muslim
Note; Rising from the ashes of Atheism, and Communism.

Argentina

Government ; Republic
GDP; per capita, $9,700
Literacy Rate 96%
Religion; Christian, Roman Catholic
Note; Although this nation is termed a republic,
it is known for its dictatorial government regimes.

Saudi Arabia

Government ; Monarchy with council of ministers.
GDP; per capita, $ 10,300
Literacy Rate 63%
Religion; Muslim 100%
Note; The population is 21,500,000. This
country is the largest exporter of petroleum in the world.
The government rules with an iron hand. The penalty for stealing is
the loss of a hand.
The penalty for conversion to Christianity is death.
The GDP is exaggerated because of little
industry required to produce crude oil. The
royal family controls the wealth.

Iran

Government; Islamic Republic. A theocratic dictatorship.
GDP; per capita, $5,500
Literacy Rate; 79%
Religion; Muslim about 99% {Radical}.Freedom
is being demanded as the populace is more exposed
to western culture.

India

Government, Federal Republic
GDP; per capita, $1,600
Literacy Rate; 52%
Religion; Hindu 80%; Muslim 14%
Population; over a billion
Poverty stricken, with abundant
natural resources.

China

Government, Communist.
GDP; per capita, $3,400
Literacy Rate; 82%
Religion; Officially Atheist

Nigeria

Government, Republic.
GDP; per capita, $1,300
Literacy Rate; 57%
Religion; Muslim 50%, Christian 40%

Israel

Government; Republic
GDP. per capita; $17,500
Literacy Rate; 96%
Religion; Judaism 82%, Muslim 14%

Liberia

Government; Republic
GDP; per capita $1,000
Literacy Rate; 38%
Religion; Traditional Beliefs, 70%
Muslim, Christian.
Population; 3,000,000
This nation was founded by
U.S. black freedmen in 1822

The United States Of America

Government; Federal Republic
GDP; $30,200
Literacy Rate; 97%
Religion; predominately Christian
Population; 272,640,000

The major religions, other than Christianity;

Buddhism

Founded 525 BC, by Guatemala Siddmartha, enlightenment achieved by intense meditation. The sacred text is the Triptaka, a collection of Buddha's teachings.

The organization is the Sanha's monastic order. The practice varies widely according to sect, { austere, meditation to magical chanting}. Elaborate temple Rites. Exorcism of devils.

Beliefs: Life is misery and decay, and there is no ultimate reality in it, or beyond it. The endless cycle of birth and rebirth, because of a desire and attachment to unreal self.

Right meditation and deeds will end the cycle and achieve Nirvana, the void, the nothingness.

There are about 326,275,000 Buddhists in the world.

Hinduism

Founded about 500 BC by Aryan invaders of India, where their vedic religion mixed with the practices and beliefs of the natives.

The sacred text; The vedo, including the Upanishads, a collection of rituals and mythological and philosophical commentaries, which includes a vast number of epic stories about gods, heroes, and saints.

Organization: None. Rituals are performed by or assisted by the priestly caste. However anyone can perform the rituals.

Brahmins are the final Judges. A variety of private rituals are used. There is no concept of orthodoxy in Hinduism. This presents a variety of sects, most of them devoted to the worship of one of the many gods, {Vishnu,, Shiva, and the goddess Shakty.

Beliefs; There is only one living principle. The many gods are aspects of the unity. Life with its many forms appears to be a separation from the divine, a meaningless cycle of birth and rebirth,{Amsard}, determined by purity of past deeds. To improve one's Karma, or escape, {Samsara}, by pure acts, thoughts. and or devotion is the aim of every Hindu.

There are about 93,076,000 Hindus in the world.

Islam

Founded about 622 AD; at Mecca.

Founder; Muhammad the Prophet and statesman.

Sacred Text; Koran, the Word of God, describing what Muhammad said or did

Organization; Muslim leadership has combined the civil, and the moral function of the state.

There are cultural and national groups held together by a common religious law, the Shari'a, enforced uniformly in the matters of religion only.

Practice; Besides the moral law, there are five pillars of Islam

1-Profession of faith

2-Oneness of God.

3-Priesthood of Muhammad

4-Prayer, five times a day.

5-Alms from one's savings, and estate

Dawn to dusk fasting in the month of Remadan. Once in a lifetime pilgrimage to Mecca.

Divisions; The Sunni, and the Shiites. The Shiites believe in twelve Imams { teachers after Muhammad}, who have become invisible since 874 who continue to teach the community. The Sunni believe in God's overpowering control in all things, all is predestined.

Beliefs; Strictly monotheistic, God is the creator, and the center of the universe, omnipotent, omniscient, just, forgiving, and merciful. The human is God's greatest creation, but is weak and egocentric, prone to forget the goal of life.

God revealed the Koran to Muhammad. to guide humanity to truth and justice. Those who repent and sincerely submit, {The literal meaning of Islam}, to God, attain salvation. The forgiven enter paradise, and the wicked burn in Hell.

They believe that Jesus was a prophet of God.

The believers are told to spread the Word of Muhammad around the world, preferably by teaching, but by the sword if necessary.

It is the fastest growing religion in the world today. There are about 1,126,325,000 Muslims living in the Middle East, and around the world. They offer a structured life of following.

It appears, that Muhammad borrowed considerably from the teachings of Christ, which has a redeeming effect of love.

The church and state are basically one, creating an oppressive force, depriving one of free speech, and action, through a subtle threat of punishment.

Regarding the above nations and their religions, none appear to be searching for the absolute truth.

Truth is an absolute, and the closer we are to it, the more healthy, vibrant, caring, loving and materially wealthy we will be, because our thinking and attitudes will be in accordance with the laws of our being.

Our people are told by the all-knowing in the Washington Loop that our taxes are lower than other countries, so be grateful. Others in the Loop tell us that we should follow the pattern of the more progressive nations. After looking at the above; Which one?

DRUGS

It has been said of old, "Where there is a demand, there will be a supply". Another adage states, "Find a need and fill it". Both of these cliche`s are basically good for anyone who wishes to become successful in business. How utterly simple, just find a need and find a way to fill it. Simple, not easy. If one sees a demand for a product or a service, simply meet the demand. If one sees a possibility of creating a potential demand and a way of meeting it, he or she can become extremely wealthy especially in a wealthy country of hedonists, and their counterparts, the very poor. Those with money are looking for kicks, and the poor are looking for a way out of reality.

Regarding the above two clichés, the first is in reference to need, and the second is in reference to want. There is a vast difference between the two.

Farmers grow food to fill a need. They also grow tobacco to fill a want. They grow corn and other grain to fill a need. They also grow corn and other grain to fill a want in the form of whiskey.

In the countries of Columbia, Peru, Bolivia, Ecuador, and the countries of Asia, Syria, Israel, the farmers grow crops for food, and they also grow poppies, hemp. and coca plants. They sell their so-called internationally illegal crops to places like Columbia, Syria, etc. where they are processed into the dream potions. And then shipped to Mexico where it is smuggled into the U.S, and other prosperous western nations populated with generally speaking, well to do citizens with high hedonistic wants. Much of the raw materials for the illegal drugs come from countries where if a citizen is caught partaking of the finished product they are executed or have their hands cut off.

The scope of the problem is world wide, with friendly and enemy nations involved. The real problem is demand. If it were bread it could be understood, but the hell on earth caused by a demand for a temporary fix of a deadly feel good substance, which causes addiction is difficult for reasonable persons to understand. This affliction is not of nature, but the result of a percentage of citizens who will defy all reason to perpetuate their demand for fun.

The United States is becoming involved in the civil war in Columbia. Our country has committed billions of dollars in aid. The aid consists of military personnel, equipment, training, financing, intelligence. Also included are 60 transport and attack helicopters. The American people are told that it has to do with crop control, especially the coca crop that provides at least 90% of the cocaine that reaches the American market.

We are at war with about 17,000 strong forces of Marxist insurgency in the civil war which is now in its fourth decade. This war has killed 35,000 people, and displaced 2,000,000 persons. Do the makers of U.S. policy understand the long simmering stew of class conflict, ideological war, and ethnic vendettas that is raging in this stricken country? This little mess could become a tar baby from which we find we can not escape. All this for a percentage of weak minded individuals who demand that their wants be met.

The administration advertises their policy as drug control through crop extermination. The left wing forces control one half of the country of Columbia and are getting hundreds of millions of dollars per year protecting and taxing the coca fields.

The U.S. policy is peace through herbicides, and its aim is to neutralize the left-wing forces by impoverishing them. As a result the insurgents, armed with automatic rifles and personal computers, stop traffic, check motorists' bank records, then detain any-one whose family may be able to afford a lucrative ransom. There is on the average of seven kidnappings per day.

Exercising the most wild dream, and belief, that if the U.S. is successful in eradicating the coca crop in Columbia, would be the end of the problems with drugs is bordering on a complete loss of circumspect. If Columbia is made clean, cultivation of the coca plant would increase in other neighboring countries.

In spite of Columbia's national effort to take back their country from the Marxists rebels, coca cultivation has increased 140% in the last five years, and this occurred because the U.S. financed the Bolivian reduction in coca cultivation.

The greater the effort in Columbia will result in the growers to spread their cultivation into other adjoining nations. There is so little chance of successfully eradicating the curse of drug addiction simply because of the tremendous profits to be had in the illegal field of supplying demand.

The coca plant growers, and the converting plant owners, and the smugglers are a bloodthirsty combination of criminals who terrify the governments of the countries in which they operate.

Is it plausible to think that the U.S. can police every South American country, and supply aid?

Will the United States ever learn? With a $50,000,000,000 annual demand for an easily smuggled product made in poor countries, the demand will be met.

The United States of America has many enemies in the world who would like nothing better than to see this country fall. Even at the risk of killing the goose that is laying the golden eggs, some of these fanatical governments would try. They cannot do this militarily but they sure can by immobilizing the nation with drugs that create a mindset of not caring, and escape.

In the nineteenth century the mighty nations of the world were in the process of building empires, including the U.S.. They established zones in China which they declared their centers of influence. They exploited the natural resources, and the people to the limit. Now and again there would be an uprising against these practices by the people. The plundering nations used the poppy plant to subdue the dissenters in the form of opium, made from morphine which was made from the poppy.

This practice provoked anger among the leaders, those who could not stand by and see their country pillaged by foreigners. They organized among themselves and called their organization the Boxers. In 1900 they revolted against any authority and created what is known as the Boxer revolution. They confiscated the properties of the marauders, and murdered many of the company representatives in the most brutal fashion. The marauders sent their military which by sheer numbers, and modern equipment overcame the insurgents.

Maybe some of these developing nations remember what drugs can do.

What we have seen in the above space is really less than the tip of the iceberg. Columbia is mentioned because it appears in the press as though it is the only country involved. This epidemic of drugs is world spread, and spreading. There is hardly a nation that is not involved with this scourge that devastates so many lives.

Young people use drugs not because they are bad, but because of peer pressure. This pressure is real and mighty and is very difficult to resist regardless of parental guidance, or even the law. The young people believe as we all believed at one time, that they are invincible, they will live forever, and are perfectly capable of making their own decisions. To them the older generation has just emerged from the dark ages, so how could they understand the demands of their day. How possibly could they understand the excitement of the raging hormones and the desire to satisfy them.

Young people thrive on excitement, and one way to experience excitement is to experiment in drugs, sex, or anything else their young and energy filled bodies desire.

In a recent study it was found that the front lobal areas of the brain which control reasoning does not develop fully until a person reaches the age of 21 or older. If this be the case are we going to label these children who partake, criminals? Are we going to label these children who are in a sense victims, criminals, and send them to jail for possession, and hang a criminal record around their necks for the rest of their lives?

At one time even without speaking the words, was the wisdom that , the young person wants to set the world on fire, and it takes the older person to keep them from doing it. Of course today age with its wisdom is despised and the young are leading the parade even as heads of the governmental agencies.

The very sad result of experimenting with drugs is when these young people who believed that they were invincible become hooked and become desperate for a fix. This craving to satisfy the pain of body and soul forces them to become pushers and involve other young people using drugs. Or they may turn to criminal activities to secure money to satisfy their habit.

After all is said and done however these young people are partly the cause for this worldwide scourge, which today encourages criminality around the world because of the huge profits to be had in dealing drugs.

In addition to the above are the middle class seniors whose frontal lobe areas are very slow in developing who use drugs as they have so sophisticatedly termed, recreational.

Then last but certainly not least are the poor in spirit, and poor in material needs who live in the urban areas of the large cities who partake of the nectar of the gods to escape the misery of their existence. Drugs are the joy of life, they enable one to live in another world of happy dreams simply by a quick fix. Of course one has to pay the fiddler, and when you do not have the money, your addiction will force you to get it by good means or foul.

Yes, all groups of users are the cause of this horrible epidemic of drugs and crime all over the world. However, the question must be asked; Are these people, the users, criminals or victims? They are a mixture of both.

What is the driving force of the illegal drug industry? All would agree that it is big money, very big money. Who gets all of this money? Some of those receiving this big money are in high places in government, in big business, in small businesses, in local police jurisdictions.

What has our federal government done about this disease which is threatening the welfare of the nation? It has legislated against the use of these many feel good potions. What has our federal government accomplished? Nothing, the epidemic is widening, it is growing in spite of the statistics they are constantly showering upon the citizens everyday.

They appoint Drug Czars ever so often, and every one of these Czars guarantees that he or she will eradicate this curse forever, but it gets worse.

Here are a few of the statistics given to the public, which are up to date: FACT AND FIGURES, from the office of The National Drug Control Policy.http://www, whitehousedrugpolicy, gov/

New drugs are being introduced at a rapid rate. Here are just a few. These are CLUB DRUGS. M.D.M.A./ Ecstasy, Rohypnol, GHB, Ketaamine. These drugs are popular among the young teens, and young adults. They are the in thing to do drugs. These drugs make it possible for the youngsters to attend parties and dance all night without resting. They are often used to encourage date rape because they tranquilize. These drugs are of the same substance used on animals, as they produce hallucinatory effects similar to PCP and LSD.

Prevalence Estimates; Among high school students surveyed in 1999, 5.6% of 12th graders, 4.4% of 10th graders, and 1.7% of the eighth graders stated that they had used MDMA in the past year, 6.8% of college students and 7.2% of young adults [ages 19–28] surveyed in 1998 reported that they had used MDMA at least once in their lifetimes. 3.9% of college students and 2.9% of young adults reported to have used MDMA in the past year. The greatest number of users were in the 18-25 year group.

Consequences of Use; Using MDMA can cause serious psychological and physical damage. The psychological effects can include confusion, depression, anxiety. and paranoia and may last weeks after ingesting MDMA. It can also cause muscle breakdown and kidney, and cardiovascular system failure.

This is but one of the illegal drugs that are ravishing our young people. To elaborate on the others would simply be a work of dramatization, and soon forgotten along with the other boring statistics. The reader can read the 98 pages of the report found in the web site shown above.

What is being done to eradicate this scourge? Quite a bit. The D.E.A. has seen an increase in the number of arrests and seizures of MDMA. The D.E.A. seized over 950,000 tablets in 1999. All of the club drugs have been scheduled under the Controlled Substances Act.

There has been 32 agencies, or expanded offices of old agencies thrown into the war against drugs, along with the Army, the Navy, the Coast Guard, the law enforcement departments in every town, village, city, county, and state.

In addition to the above we have the Mission Statements of ONDCP Component Offices; Bureau of State and Local Affairs, The Counterdrug Technology Center, the Office of Demand Reduction, The office of Intelligence , the Office of Legal Counsel, the office of Legislative Affairs, the office of Programs, Budget, Research and Evaluation, and the Public Affairs Office and finally the office of Supply Reduction.

Other agencies such as the Drug Enforcement Administration, Federal Bureau of Investigation, the Customs Service of the U.S. Coast Guard NNICC, the Department of State, the Department of Defense, Internal Revenue Service, Central Intelligence Agency, National Institute on Drug Abuse Immigration and Naturalization Service Office, National Drug Control Policy National Narcotics Intelligence Consumers. These are all under the Department of Justice.

Again what has been accomplished? In 1996 a concerted drug law enforcement caused a change in operations, which resulted in setbacks with the arrests, surrender, or death of key leaders in the Cali Drug Mafia. The Shan United Army in the Far East collapsed, and Khun Sa was detained by the Burmese central authorities.

However in the meanwhile just to our south, drug gangs in Mexico transported cocaine to the United States, and increased their involvement in U.S. domestic cocaine distribution. They continued to produce not only heroin and marijuana, but increasingly, methamphetamine for the U.S. market. Couriers controlled by West African criminals continued to flood through U.S. airports with high -quality Southeast Asian heroin, and South American heroin suppliers increased their U.S. market share, particularly along the East Coast of the United States.

Again in the meanwhile Columbia-based mafias continued to dominate all aspects of the cocaine trade, from acquisition of cocaine base to cocaine production in South America, and transportation of the drugs to wholesale distribution in the United States. These mafias continue to operate even though their top leaders are incarcerated. They control through family on the outside.

Potential cocaine production was estimated by the U.S. Government to be 760 metric tons. The Federal Law Enforcement Agencies seized 108 metric tons of cocaine in Fiscal Year 1996. Where did the rest go? It went into the arms and legs, into the nose, and into the stomachs of our young people who are the hope of our future. This is no longer cute, it is a tragedy happening, and will continue to happen until someone has the intestinal fortitude to do something about it. Why does the government continue to use the same old tired methods they know do not work, they not only do not work the epidemic is worsening.

Now opium production is on the rise. In 1996 it was estimated that opium production was 4,285 metric tons, an increase over 1995 by 120 metric tons. Opium can easily be converted into cocaine depending on the availability of transportation.

Nationally, in the first half of 1996, Southeast Asian heroin ranged in price from $95,000 to $210,000 per kilogram. A kilogram equals about 2.2 pounds, that is about 35.2 ounces, or 1000 grams. Heroin from Southwest Asia is priced at $80,000 to $260,000 per kilogram. The price is determined by purity of the drug, where it is sold, and the demand.

At $100 per gram, times 1000 grams per kilogram=$100,000. When we multiply the gram by 1000 we arrive at 1,000,000,000 mg:'s, at what the market can extort per mg.

The gram price is determined by the demand, the purity and its source. The greater number hooked, the higher the price can go.

Methamphetamine trafficking and abuse in the United States have been on the rise over the past few years. As a result this drug is having a devastating impact in many communities across the nation. This drug is becoming the drug of choice over cocaine in many areas. Mexico has become the hub of manufacture and distribution into the U.S.. Historically this drug was associated with white males between the ages of 19 and 40 It is now becoming popular among women, college students, and young professionals at all-night parties.

During 1996 , a typical price for one gram of Methamphetamine was $45 in San Diego, and in Kansas City, Missouri $100. This is the drug that supplies a false sense of power, and allows one to party all night without resting. This is what some of our $10,000,000 per year athletes use to keep fit. It is also used in the Olympics to disqualify some of the most talented athletes.

Volumes could be written on the subject telling of the horrors, the lives lowered into the cesspool, lost forever. We seldom hear of the men who are stressed out, coming home and closing the garage door and smoking marijuana, separating themselves from their families. They have traded their families for dope. Mothers and Fathers trade their children for dope. Men and Women trade their careers for dope.

What can be done to eradicate this epidemic? With the full force of the nation's military, and bureaucracies, only feeble results have been achieved. When an operation is shut down in one area of the country another starts up in another area. When one type of drug is reduced another comes onto the market. In the meantime our citizens are paying a tremendous price in taxes for so little results. If the results up to date reduced the supply to any degree the money would be well spent, but it hasn't. Young people are dropping out of school to become wealthy very fast entering the drug market.

One kilogram=2.2 lbs. Therefore 2.2lbs=35.2 ounces. One kilogram= 1000 grams. One gram=1000 mg. What the dosage of the typical user is, is unknown. It all depends upon the amount of kick he or she desires. The number of fixes per average user is unknown, because again it is up to the user. The longer the addiction the more fixes are needed per day.

The nickel bag can be had for as low as $5.00 The amount of drug in this fix is determined by the pusher. The range is out of all proportions. There are as high as 9.8 million users. If the user uses only one mg. per fix the value at retail would be $1,000,000 per kilogram. These numbers are mind boggling, and when young people are addicted to them it is truly a calamity.

Again, what is being done about it by our government? With the billions of dollars being spent, and the man hours wasted, the answer is not much. Why? Because there is nothing that can be done about it until the use is stopped, and this is impossible as has been proven over these so many years. The users are the criminals, and at the same time they are weak minded adults, and the immature children victims. There will always be this element.

If we cannot stop the use, then we must stop the supply. This too is impossible, because of the high profits. The criminal element with their clever minds will find a way to fill the demand even if that means pushing dope onto elementary school children and have them push dope onto their classmates. There is no depth that this criminal element won't go to make their millions. They are clever, and use their cleverness to devise ways to transport drugs into this country. With all the seizures we hear about by the governmental agencies, it is truly only a small fraction of the whole.

Again, What is the Answer?
Be Honest.
The Answer is Legalize Drugs

Oh, how it hurts to face the truth.

Now comes the torrent of emotions which have swept away reason for so many years. There now comes the question of what will happen to the younger generation when they can buy drugs on the open market? A quick answer would be that they can buy all the drugs they want on the illicit market now. However we are not looking for a cute answer, nor a such a quick fix for such a serious problem.

First the benefits of legalized drugs should be considered.

The only thing that keeps the illicit drug locomotive going is money. Stop the profits and you stop the drug trade dead in its tracks. It is as easy as that. It is utterly ridiculous to legislate against morals, and that is what this problem is all about. This nation discovered that when the 18th amendment became law.

What would happen if the drug trade was eradicated?

1-The mad rush to build prisons would cease, saving billions of dollars. We are not talking money here, we are talking about the saving of the reputations of thousands of addicted souls by eliminating the curse of a being a felon.

2- The police would no longer have to spend time arresting drug users. They would have more time to give to the work they are good at doing, that is keeping the peace and protecting the neighborhood. They would not have to arrest a pusher in the morning and see him released two hours later because of a close tie he has with some influential personage, who may be involved in the business. The policeman would not jeopardize his life dealing with madmen.

3-There would be no need for SWAT teams crashing into crack houses because there would not be any.

4-Children would not be enticed to enter the drug world and make all of that easy money, which necessitates their belonging to a criminal gang.

5-The present users would not have to sell themselves on the streets to support their habit.

6-Elementary school children would not be pushed by the pushers to sell drugs to their classmates in order to addict them and create a market for the pushers.

7-The Army and Navy could go back to the purpose of their being.

8-The thousands of bureaucrats who have been for years sitting, shuffling paper, and attending meetings, making up reports, telling their superiors what a good job they are doing in controlling drugs in this town and that town, would have to find work elsewhere. The savings in dollars would be sufficient to open half way houses for the treatment for drug abuse alone, free of charge.

9-The nation would be rid of a criminal element imported with the illicit drugs. We as a nation may sense a feeling of cleanliness, and stability again when the pushers who have encouraged addiction and laughed at the law are made immobile, or have left the country.

10-Last but not least legalizing drugs will eliminate the excitement of the undeveloped mind of young people, and possibly the immature adults of being of the in-crowd who thrive on being different. In other words it would eliminate peer pressure to experiment if it was legal. At that age to do anything legal is being a nerd.

During the days of prohibition of the selling or using alcoholic beverages, the young of that day would not be caught dead without a silver plated flask, curved to fit around the rib cage, and carried around in the inner jacket pocket. In those good ole days when the young were sure that they had all of the answers, they would carry the flasks into the speakeasies and pour their alcohol into the set-ups supplied by the night club owner.

When the stupid amendment was overturned, the flasks were relegated to an empty drawer or were saved as souvenirs, but were never carried again.

Alcohol addiction is caused in many cases by peer pressure experimentation.

Tobacco addiction is caused in many cases by peer pressure experimentation.

Drug addiction is caused in just about every case by peer pressure experimentation.

The first two addictions are bad, but they do not devastate lives so quickly as the third, and they at least give the user a chance to see the folly of their ways and with some willpower and a little help they can overcome. Not so with drugs. They enslave the body, soul, mind, strength, they ravish, then kill.

Legalizing drugs will not eliminate all temptation. There will always be plenty of things of which one can become a slave.

To legalize drugs to the extent that they could be bought at any grocery store, drug store, or service station would be a calamity waiting to happen. Drugs as well as alcohol, and tobacco are controlled substances. This being the case then they must be controlled.

They can be controlled by each state as is done in North Carolina. They have state liquor stores where anyone of age can purchase any alcoholic beverage.

Drugs can be sold the same way. Anyone of age can purchase the drug of his or her choice, with no questions asked, except proof of age. There would be one major difference, the drugs sold would be bought from legitimate drug makers at a price which would be only a very small fraction of the illicit drug price. The state would add to that price the cost of the physical building from which the drug is sold, and the employees who would be employed by the state.

The cost to the user would be the cost of production in huge amounts which would lower the cost., and the cost of selling. There would not be any profit for any entity involved. The legal age could be decided upon, possibly 18 to 21 years of age. Anyone purchasing drugs and supplying anyone under the legal age would be imprisoned as a 2nd degree murderer. If a new drug is introduced, the state would have it analyzed and duplicate it, and sell it in the store. Once again the cost to the user would be only a fraction of what is now being paid on the street for poor grade poison There would be no temptation to sell drugs illegally because there would not be a profit, and why would anyone risk being arrested for a 2nd degree murder charge for no profit. It is the risk that raises the prices to the addicted.

It has been wisely stated that, the devil is in the detail. This failed drug policy will not be retired and a new concept be introduced on these few pages. This issue would naturally have to be brought up in the committees of the legislative bodies of the government, and the details negotiated. However this issue must be raised in the legislature and acted upon promptly. Every day means more of our children and immature adults are being pushed to their doom by a gang of bloodthirsty monsters whose aim is to conquer the heart and soul of America for a profit.

The only reason that legislation will not be applied to this issue is if people high in government positions, or those who support them have already been bought with a price. If this be the case then the only hope is in the citizenry, or have they too been bought with the price for their apathy.

For instance, in a newspaper article in The Tribune, on page 3-a, not on the front page, dated 10/5/00, and written by Lance Gay of Scripps Howard News Agency, quite a reliable source, this headline was found ; " **DRUG CZAR'S OFFICE PROBED**". The article goes on; " Congressional investigators opened a criminal investigation of the White House drug czar's office this spring after uncovering *EVIDENCE* that contractors have inflated advertising costs for the $1,000,000,000 national anti-drug campaign".

Robert Hast, head of the congressional G.A.O. states that its auditors uncovered evidence involving an estimated $8,000,000 in inflated charges involving government contracts. The charges involve inflated billing for work done on the antidrug contracts, payments of bonuses to executives, improper travel charges. This charge is made against the giant advertising firm of Ogilvy & Mather. A former employer has informed the G.A.O. of other improprieties.

Mr. Hast stated that his investigation was hindered by White House appointed DRUG CZAR BARRY McCAFFREY, this spring, who refused to allow auditors to complete an audit of the drug office contracts.

This is only the tip of the proverbial iceberg. If the public only knew the rest of the story of fraud, greed, cover-up, and politics involved in this phony, inept, ridiculous, life sucking department, they would rise up in the streets, not only the radical, but the decent citizens of this country, and demand an immediate closing down of this insidious, fake Office of the Drug Czar.

The above opens the window a trifle to the reason that this department continues to exist.

We the pubic must be heard loud and clear, not muffled by political correctness which is used to keep us quiet, and do what we are told.

Begin it and the mind will be heated,

Start it and the work will be completed.

Or take what is left.

Only the truth can give us the answer that will prevail. Do we any longer have the intestinal fortitude to stand up and be counted?

In the name of all that is decent, end this present fraud ridden drug policy.

This curse is a moral problem, not a political problem. Morals can never, never, never be legislated successfully.

Alcohol, and tobacco are harmful substances, and addictive, and their sales are controlled. Why not do the same with drugs? By so doing we can save many of this generation and more in the next.

WHAT IS LEFT?

What is it that we all seek? Some will answer; happiness. However happiness is the byproduct of something else. Others may answer; peace of mind, others freedom. However freedom can only be retained by eternal vigilance. What do we have? We have apathy. This huge economic giant of a nation with all of its wonderful people has become a nation of fighting tribes, tribes trying to get theirs first. They are not a bit interested in the general overall welfare of the country in which they live, as though it did not matter what happens to America so long as they get theirs. Some call this rugged individuality, or the American dream, or the pursuit of happiness. It could be plutomania, a mad desire for great wealth. A form of insanity. We coped with the great depression, and the great wars, but we just can't cope with great opportunity, or the respite from the anxiety of want.

Let us analyze the word happiness. The dictionary defines it as, favored by circumstance, lucky, fortunate. However true happiness is found in a feeling of well being, brought about by right thinking. Freedom means not to be under the control or power of another, able to act or think without arbitrary restrictions, having liberty, be independent.

Seeking happiness as a goal in life is a modern concept. Before the American revolution, people of the world were not too happiness conscious, they were more food and shelter conscious. They married for financial considerations of the parents. The churches through demagoguery threatened the uneducated by charging so much a step out of purgatory, and the truth was hidden in the dark recesses of superstition. The church and the state were one.

It was not until July 4th, 1776, when these wonderful words were spoken and written, that the beautiful beams of hope of happiness, and freedom came within the realm of possibility.

"WHEN, IN THE COURSE OF HUMAN EVENTS, IT BECOMES NECESSARY FOR ONE PEOPLE TO DISSOLVE THE POLITICAL BANDS WHICH HAVE CONNECTED THEM WITH ANOTHER, AND TO ASSUME, AMONG THE POWERS OF THE EARTH, THE SEPARATE AND EQUAL STATION TO WHICH THE LAWS OF NATURE AND OF NATURES' GOD ENTITLE THEM, A DECENT RESPECT TO THE OPINIONS OF MANKIND REQUIRES THAT THEY SHOULD DECLARE THE CAUSES WHICH IMPEL THEM TO THE SEPARATION".

NEW PRINCIPLES OF GOVERNMENT

"WE HOLD THESE TRUTHS TO BE SELF EVIDENT; THAT ALL MEN ARE CREATED EQUAL, THAT THEY ARE ENDOWED BY THEIR CREATOR WITH CERTAIN UNALIENABLE RIGHTS, THAT AMONG THESE ARE LIFE, LIBERTY, AND THE PURSUIT OF HAPPINESS.

The above is not taken from the Democrat Party, or the Republican Party platforms, they were taken from the inspired minds of those who knew the despots of the world, and how these despots smothered the people, killed their spirits, and made slaves of them. These men who were so inspired, as to risk life, and personal possessions to bring about the rising of the sun of freedom, created a nation which truly became the hope of the world, the cradle of possibility for all human beings regardless of race, creed, or nationality.

Note the above; WE HOLD THESE TRUTHS to be self evident. There was no doubt in the minds of the founding fathers that the NEW PRINCIPLES OF GOVERNMENT were truths revealed by the wisdom of the ages, and not the political correctness of the day. These truths were self evident, they were the inherent rights of mankind. Given at the time of conception when an individual life begins. These rights are not alien they are not from a different planet. They were given through grace by the Creator, not the government.

What were these truths?

#1All men are created equal, and endowed by their Creator with certain unalienable rights.{not the government]

It is almost impossible to believe what our people have been politically corrected to completely distort the meaning of this declaration. Certain self interest groups are doing their best to persuade the nation that the term means that the government is established to make men equal.

This thought pattern is utterly ridiculous, it shows immaturity, wishful thinking, and encourages self pity, and lack of ambition, not setting goals, or accomplishing much of anything in life, because one believes that they are at a disadvantage, they are handicapped, and should be taken care of by someone.

Although promised by our politicians that they will equalize everything, and make us all the same, it is impossible to do. Who in the world in their right mind can say that all mankind is or ever can be equal in the physical, or mental realm?

A man's stature effects his image as a leader. Can a government make a short man, tall? A woman's beauty effects her course in a career, or in the world of sexual sparring. Can the government make a woman more attractive? Can anyone deny that some of us have a higher I.Q. than others, and lower than some? Can the government with all the power of its coffers raise one's intelligent quotient whether it be a man or woman? Can we say that the boy or girl raised in a family of profanity, drunkenness, and drug dependence has an equal chance of success in life? Can a government step into the home and arrest the mother and father for being irresponsible parents, and put the children in foster care, managed by the government and all of the ramifications of that move, and still claim equality for the children?

These questions could be carried to just about the most ridiculous extent, as the thought pattern that provoked them.

All men and women are created equal in the sight of the Creator, and all men and women has been given by their Creator the equal right to opportunity, and the freedom to pursue those things that will enrich their lives in all aspects of being, regardless of their physical prowess, or their intelligent quotient No person regardless of creed, color, national origin, or religious faith should be deprived in any way, of the unalienable rights, the God given rights to life, liberty, and the pursuit of happiness.

Allow all men and women to become the best they can be, regardless of their deficiencies or their genius. It is about time that the American people are given a reprieve from the constant bombardment of propaganda, that to be rich is a sin. In the majority of cases rich people who own much of this world's goods have a talent to do this, and this is their way of pursuing happiness.   There is one thing sure, and that is, not all of the happy campers who have made it big in the financial world are happier than those who do not have the talent, but have acquired a loving peace of mind. The one per cent of the wealthiest pay about 30% of the total income tax collected, even after their CPAs have used every loophole to avoid paying. Why do our politicians divide the nation by fostering hatred between the rich and the poor? The only room for dislike would be if the rich prohibited the poor from becoming rich.

Risking the very good chance of being stereotyped a pedantic speaker or writer, let us analyze the word, "unalienable". Words are things, and mean things that are so often passed by when reading, or when the reader becomes impatient with words that are not commonly used.

As strange as it may seem, the word "unalienable" is not in the present day dictionary. The replacement word is, "Inalienable". Regardless of how the word is spelled, the meaning is the same. It means, a thing, an entity that can not be taken away. The reason is that no one gave these rights to us, no government gave these rights to us, they are inherent rights given by the Creator to all human creatures which are the epitome of His creation. This is absolute truth, from the absolute source of truth, our God in whom there is no shadow of turning. There never can be peace on earth so long as the absolute truth is not acknowledged. The world attempts to banish it, but it is the sole foundation upon which the entire creation rests. It is the wisdom of the ages, and the touchstone for knowing right from wrong in all aspects of life. Only the truth can set any of us free, and help us all to overcome ourselves.

It appears that since the beginning of recorded history governments have, constantly, either by force, or subtle maneuvering, such as political correctness, strove to remove this notion of individual freedom, simply because it is dangerous to their drive for absolute power. In this day our government is dumbing down the citizens by giving them what they call, their rights. and giving them things bought with the citizens'own money, and then say; See what we are doing for you.

In regard to Unalienable or Inalienable rights, take no man's word for it. Search your own mind and know that these rights of life, liberty, and the pursuit of happiness are as natural as breathing. Search your own heart and find the emotional verification to the reasoning of your mind.

These rights are inherent at birth. Watch the two year old begin to dominate the parents in its first battle for freedom from their authority. This battle continues through puberty, this constant battle to get from under authority. This continues even in college, when these young men and women fight the authority of the administration. They thrive on their crusade to be free, even though they forget that they are so dependent.

The right to life, liberty, and the pursuit of happiness is an absolute truth, granted by the very source of absolute truth.

Today this nation is constantly being bombarded by the post modern thinkers, or shall we say the post modern non-thinkers whose philosophy is, that there is no absolute truth, and that truth is relative, and anyone's truth is as true as anyone else's. This is a beautiful philosophy for those who declare that they want to be free, which of course means, they do not want to assume any responsibility, and go through life accomplishing nothing of substance, except being a guru for others, dancing on moonbeams.

What do we have left? We have a temporary economic boom that can evaporate very quickly because of an OPEC oil reduction, or a slowdown in the magical world of technology. Our individual savings is negative, more is owed on the credit card than is saved.

Our manufacturing jobs are being sent overseas in order to exploit the cheap labor in the third world countries, all in the name of helping them become democratic politically, and claiming that at the same time this will create jobs over here. What kind of a job will the worker find in this country if the manufacturing jobs are being shipped overseas, in case of a recession? If the worker is not a technician he will have no work, except to scrub floors. Maybe that this is the goal of the one world brain trust, the power seekers of the world.

We have a nation where the citizens look to the government for all things, and the government obliges by giving them what they think they want, and then raises taxes to pay for all of the goodies in order to pad their own nests. As a result we have the highest taxes in the history of the country except when the nation was at war.

The entire nation is buying on credit, including the goodies that are handed out as favors by the candidates. The goodies come, and then slowly but surely come the taxes, just like buying a car on time. We pay the price of the goods, and the interest in the form of budget deficits, and national debt. When will this madness cease? When will we as a nation return to what made us great in the first place? When will we be true to ourselves, and our fellow man, and become responsible citizens again, realizing that life is not a constant party, and the search for fun is for children. When will we realize that principle in character is our only hope to remain a free people?

The Garden of the Mind

A man's mind may be likened to a garden, which may be intelligently cultivated or allowed to run wild; but whether cultivated or neglected, it must and will bring forth. If no useful seeds are put into the garden, then an abundance of useless seeds will fall into it, and will produce their kind. Every man is where he is by the law of his being; the thoughts which he has built into his character have brought him there, and in the arrangement of his life there is no element of chance, but all is the result of a law which cannot err.

As a progressive and evolving being, man is where he is that he may learn that he may grow, and as he learns the spiritual lesson which any circumstance contains for him, it passes away and gives place to other circumstances.

Man is buffeted by circumstances so long as he believes himself to be the creature of outside conditions, but when he realizes that he is a creative power, and that he may command the hidden soil and seeds of his being out of which circumstances grow, he then becomes the rightful master of himself. That circumstances grow out of thought every man knows who has for any length of time practiced self-control and self-purification.

The soul attracts that which it secretly harbors; that which it loves, and also that which it fears; it reaches the height of its cherished aspirations; it falls to the levels of its unchastened desires-and circumstances are the means by which the soul receives its own. As the reaper of his own harvest, man learns both by suffering and bliss. A man does not come to the almshouse or the jail by the tyranny of fate or circumstance, but by the pathway of groveling thoughts and base desires.

Men do not attract that which they want, but that which they are.

147

The "divinity that shapes out ends is in ourselves, it is our very self. Man is manacled only by himself; thought and action are the jailers of Fate-they imprison, being base, they are also angels of Freedom-they liberate being noble.

In the light of this truth, what, then, is the meaning of "fighting against circumstances"? It means that a man is continually revolting against an effect without, while all the time he is nourishing and preserving its cause in his heart.

Men are anxious to improve their circumstances, but are unwilling to improve themselves; they therefore remain bound.

The man who does not shrink from self-crucifixion can never fail to accomplish the object upon which his heart is set. This is as true of earthly as of heavenly things.

A man can be cursed and rich; he may be blessed and poor. Blessedness and riches are only joined together when the riches are rightly and wisely used; and the poor man only descends into wretchedness when he regards his lot as a burden unjustly imposed.

A man only becomes a man when he ceases to whine and revile, and commences to seek for the hidden justice that regulates his life.

As he builds, adapts his mind to that regulating factor, he ceases to accuse others as the cause of his condition, and builds himself up in strong and noble thoughts; and ceases to kick against circumstances, but begins to use them as aids to his more rapid progress, and as a means of discovering the hidden powers and possibility within himself.

Law, not confusion, is the dominating principle in the universe, justice, not injustice, is the soul and substance of life, and righteousness, not corruption, is the molding and moving force in the spiritual government in the world. This being true, man has but to right himself to find that the universe is right, and during the process of putting himself right, he will find that as he alters his thoughts toward things. and other people, things and other people will alter toward him.

"You will be what you will to be
Let failure find its false content
In that poor word environment,
But spirit scorns it and is free.

It masters time, it conquers space,
It cows that boastful trickster chance,
And bids the tyrant circumstance,
Uncrown and fill a servant's place.

The human will, that force unseen,
The offspring of a deathless soul,
Can hew a way to any goal.
Though walls of granite intervene.

Be not impatient in delay.
But wait as one who understands;
Where spirit rises and commands.
The gods are ready to obey.

Until thought is linked with purpose there is no intelligent accomplishment. With the majority the bark of thought is allowed to drift upon the ocean of life. Aimlessness is a vice, and such drifting must not continue for him who would steer clear of catastrophe and destruction.

They who have no central purpose in their life fall an easy prey to petty worries, fears, troubles, and self-pitying, all of which are indications of weakness, which lead, just as surely as deliberately planned to failure, unhappiness, and loss, for weakness cannot persist in a power-evolving universe.

The weakest soul, knowing its own weakness, and believing this truth-that strength can only be developed by effort and practice, will, thus believing at once begin to exert itself, and, adding effort to effort, patience to patience, and strength to strength, will never cease to develop, and will at last grow divinely strong.

The will to do springs from the knowledge that we can do. Doubt and fear are the great enemies of knowledge, and he who encourages them, who does not slay them thwarts himself at every step. He who conquered doubt and fear has conquered failure.

Thought allied fearlessly to purpose becomes creative force: he who knows this is ready to become something higher and stronger than a mere bundle of wavering thought and fluctuating sensations; he who does this has become the conscious and intelligent wielder of his mental powers.

All that a man achieves and all that he fails to achieve is the direct result of his own thoughts. In a justly ordered universe, where loss of equipoise would mean total destruction, individual responsibility must be absolute.

A man's weakness and strength, purity and impurity, are his own, and not another man's; they are brought about by himself, and not by another; and they can only be altered by himself, never another. His condition is also his own, and not another man's.

His sufferings, and his happiness are evolved from within. As a man thinkest so is he; as he continues to think; so he remains.

It has been usual for men to think and to say, "many men are slaves because one is an oppressor; let us hate the oppressor". Now, however, there is among an increasing few a tendency to reverse this judgment, and to say, "One man is the oppressor because many are slaves, let us despise the slaves." The truth is that oppressor and slave are cooperators in ignorance, and. while seeming to afflict each other, are in reality afflicting themselves. A perfect knowledge perceives the action of law in the weakness of the oppressed and the misapplied power of the oppressor; a perfect Love, seeing the suffering which both states entail; condemns neither; a perfect Compassion embraces both oppressor and the oppressed.

Before a man can achieve anything , even in worldly things, he must lift his thoughts above slavish animal indulgence. He may not, in order to succeed, give up all animality and selfishness, by any means; but a portion of it must, at least be sacrificed.

The universe does not favor the greedy, the dishonest, the vicious, although on the mere surface it may sometimes appear to do so; it helps the honest. the magnanimous, the virtuous. All the great Teachers of the ages have declared this in varying form, and to prove and know it a man has but to persist in making himself more and more virtuous by lifting up his thoughts.

Spiritual achievements are the consummation of holy aspirations. He who lives constantly in the conception of noble and lofty thoughts, who dwells upon all that is pure and unselfish, will as surely as the sun reaches the zenith and the moon its full, become wise and noble in character, and rise into a position of influence and blessedness.

The dreamers are the saviors of the world. As the visible world is sustained by the invisible, so men, through all their trials and sins and sordid vocations, are nourished by the beautiful visions of their solitary dreamers. Humanity cannot forget its dreamers, it cannot let their ideals fade and die; it lives in them; it knows them as the realities which; it shall one day see and know.

Composer, sculptor, painter, poet. prophet, sage, these are the makers of the afterworld, the architects of heaven. The world is beautiful because they have lived; without them, laboring would perish.

To desire is to obtain; to aspire is to achieve. The greatest achievement was at first and for a time a dream. The oak sleeps in acorn, the bird waits in the shell; and in the highest vision of the soul a waking angel stirs. Dreams are the seedlings of realities.

And you, too, youthful reader, will realize the Vision {not the idle wish} of your heart, be it base or beautiful, or a mixture of both, for you will always gravitate toward that which you, secretly, most love. Into your hands will be placed the exact results of your own thoughts; you will receive that which you earn; no more, no less.

Whatever your present environment may be, you will fall, remain or rise with your thoughts, your Vision, your Ideal,

The thoughtless, and the indolent, seeing only the apparent effects of things and not the things themselves, talk of luck, of fortune, and chance. Seeing a man grow rich, they say, "How lucky he is !" Observing another become intellectual, they exclaim, "How highly favored he is!" They do not see the trials and the failures and struggles which these men have voluntarily encountered in order to gain their experience; have no knowledge of the sacrifices they have made, of the undaunted efforts they have put forth, of the faith they have exercised, that they might overcome the apparently insurmountable, and realize the Vision of their hearts. They do not know the darkness and the heartaches, they only see the light and joy. and call it "luck "Do not see the long and arduous journey, but only behold the pleasant goal, and call it " good fortune"; do not understand the process, but only perceive the result, and call it "chance".

Serenity

Calmness of mind is one of the beautiful jewels of wisdom. It is the result of long and patient effort in self-control. Its presence is an indication of ripened experience, and of a more than ordinary knowledge of the laws and operations of thought.

A man becomes calm in the measure that he understands himself as a thought-evolved being. for such knowledge necessitates the understanding of others as the result of thought, and as he develops a right understanding, and sees more and more clearly the internal relations of things by the action of cause and effect, he ceases to fuss and fume and worry and grieve, and remains poised, steadfast, serene.

The calm man, having learned how to govern himself, knows how to adapt himself to others, and they, in turn reverence his spirited strength and feel that they can learn of him, and rely on him.

The strong calm man is always loved and revered. He is like a shade-giving tree in a thirsty land, or a sheltering rock in a storm. Who does not like a tranquil heart, a sweet-tempered, balanced life?

That exquisite poise of character which we call serenity is the fruitage of the soul. It is precious as wisdom, more to be desired than gold-yea, than even fine gold. How insignificant mere money-seeking looks in comparison with a serene life-a life that dwells in the ocean of truth, beneath the waves, beyond the reach of tempests, in the Eternal Calm.

Yes, humanity surges with uncontrolled passion, is tumultuous with ungoverned grief, is blown about by anxiety and doubt. Only the wise man, only he whose thoughts are controlled and purified, makes the winds and the storm of the soul obey him.

Tempest- tossed souls, wherever ye may be, under whatsoever conditions ye may live, know this-in the ocean of life the isles of Blessedness are smiling, and the sunny shore of your ideas awaits your thought. Keep your hand firmly upon the helm of thought. In the bark of your soul reclines the commanding Master: He does but sleep, wake Him. Self-control is strength ; Right thought is mastery; Calmness is power. Say unto your heart, "Peace, be still !"

The above are excerpts from the jewel-filled, power- packed small book; "As a man thinketh" The author is James Allen. We should add to the title; "So is he"

The source of the wisdom of this remarkable book are the New Testament Scriptures.

These excerpts are used to create a contrast between what the world could be and what it is. They are used to show the character of the founding fathers, and the wonderful government they presented to posterity, and what the shallow thinkers, the fearful, the self-seekers, the self-pitying of the world today have left us. The contrast between our Traditions, and the Establishment of today.

It is imperative that we as citizens of this wonderful country learn and grow and again treasure character, in order to develop a sense of discernment to enable us to cast out the decay in our Nation's Capital, with its accompaning crassness, crudeness, deceit, lying, and cheapness.

There will be a revolution, either for the truth or because of the lack of it. The nation cannot any longer stand firm ruled by a streetfighter's mentality.

George Washingtion's Prayer

"Almighty God: We make our earnest prayer that Thou wilt keep the United States in Thy holy protection: that Thou wilt incline the hearts of the citizens to cultivate a spirit of subordination and obedience to government and entertain a brotherly affection and love for one another and for their fellow citizens of the Unite States at large.

And, finally, that Thou wilt most graciously be p leased to dispose us all to do justice, to love mercy, and to demean ourselves with that charity, humility, and pacific temper of mind, which were the characteristics of the Divine Author of our blessed religion, and without a humble imitation of whose example in these things we can never hope to be a happy nation.

Grant our supplications, we beseech Thee, through Jesus Christ our Lord: Amen.

About the Author

Richard Hewitt is a retired business man. He attended Johns Hopkins University, Baltimore Maryland, The Southeastern University extension college, at Martinsburg West Virginia, and attended and taught at The Wharton School of Business at the University of Pennsylvania.

During his business career he worked for a major oil company for fourteen years. He enlisted in the U.S. Army Airforce Reserves, and completed pilot training.

He has taught and published several courses in the field of Real Estate Appraising, which were approved for classroom instruction in approved State of Georgia Real Estate Schools.

His purpose in writing is his sincere desire to arouse the awareness of the potential ability that lies dormant in the hearts and minds of individual lives. As the individual is regenerated, so goes the nation and traditions.

He has through the years developed a very deep sense of discernment from the observation of the human condition, witnessing the raw needs of so many.

He is married, and has two children, and four grandchildren

WHY SHOULD ANYONE READ THIS BOOK?

Will we permit ourselves to live to the fullest, or will we choose to become abbreviated human beings? It is up to us. As we as individuals go, so goes the nation.

Nothing has been promised except equal opportunity for all.

What is the missing ingredient that causes human beings to become abbreviated? The answer is obvious to any reasonable person. It is the lack of wisdom; (wisdom is the proper use of knowledge).We have so much knowledge but so little wisdom and truth.

This book will reveal the source of all wisdom, how to approach it, and drink deeply of it for a more productive and prosperous life.

There is a great divide in our nation today between the haves and the have-nots. The have-nots being those without wisdom which is creating a cultural chasm. The chasm is widening and separating us from the traditions which made us a great nation.

It appears as though our nation no longer is able to face reality, but prefers symbolism over substance. As stated by novelist Ayn Rand; "We can evade reality, but we cannot evade the consequences of evading reality."

The final result has been a developing mob of streetfighters, of crudeness, crassness and cheapness.

There is a better way at our fingertips, and we can have it. It is our inherent right to possess it !

www.ingramcontent.com/pod-product-compliance
Lightning Source LLC
Chambersburg PA
CBHW061251280526
45784CB00002B/722